Woman's Identity and the Qur'an: A New Reading

UNIVERSITY PRESS OF FLORIDA

Florida A&M University, Tallahassee
Florida Atlantic University, Boca Raton
Florida Gulf Coast University, Ft. Myers
Florida International University, Miami
Florida State University, Tallahassee
University of Central Florida, Orlando
University of Florida, Gainesville
University of North Florida, Jacksonville
University of South Florida, Tampa
University of West Florida, Pensacola

Also by Nimat Hafez Barazangi, from the University Press of Florida

Islamic Identity and the Struggle for Justice,
edited by Nimat Hafez Barazangi, M. Raquibuz Zaman, and Omar Azfal (1996)

Woman's Identity and the Qur'an

A New Reading

Nimat Hafez Barazangi

University Press of Florida

Gainesville · Tallahassee · Tampa · Boca Raton

Pensacola · Orlando · Miami · Jacksonville · Ft. Myers

A record of cataloging-in-publication data is available
from the Library of Congress.

The University Press of Florida is the scholarly publishing agency
for the State University System of Florida, comprising Florida A&M
University, Florida Atlantic University, Florida Gulf Coast University,
Florida International University, Florida State University, University
of Central Florida, University of Florida, University of North Florida,
University of South Florida, and University of West Florida.

University Press of Florida
15 Northwest 15th Street
Gainesville, FL 32611-2079
http://www.upf.com

To Thaniyah and Husni

Contents

Preface and Acknowledgments

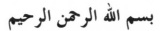

Bismi Allah Al Rahman Al Rahim
(In the name of God, the Merciful, the Compassionate)

Although the idea of this book and the research that led to it were conceived in the early 1990s, its goal has become more central than I had envisioned to the current drive toward studying Islam, Islamic education, and the role of women in "democratizing" Muslim societies. The intention and the objectives of this book are dramatically different from what has dominated the discussion of Islam and of Muslims in the last decade both within and outside the Muslim *ummah* (the universal community). The goal of *Woman's Identity and the Qur'an: A New Reading* is to generate a shift in the discourse of Islamic studies, Muslim women's studies, and Islamic pedagogy, a shift that is at once theoretical and practical. The use of the term "woman" in the singular is to emphasize the importance of self-identity and identification with the *Qur'an as the source that mandates a sine qua non shift in discourse consistent with time and place.*

The traditional and prevailing Muslim emphasis on educating the Muslim woman in order for her to play merely a complementary and domestic role contradicts Qur'anic principles and is in discord with the realities of Muslim women. The lack of Muslim woman's self-identity and identification with the Qur'an as the source for her autonomous spiritual and intellectual existence proves that such a role contradicts the Islamic principles of justice, human trusteeship (*khilafah*), and equilibrium (*taqwa*). *Taqwa* is the only criterion that differentiates individuals. The realities of most Muslim women suggest that they are not even being educated for the assumed complementary role, that is, the upbringing of Muslim children. Meanwhile, non-Muslims' emphasis on developing an emancipated Muslim woman who identifies with cultural parameters other than her own has brought only temporary solutions and does not address the core issues. By integrating a pedagogical reading and analysis of the Qur'an as well as historical synthesis of Muslim women's education in Islam, this book attempts to explain how self-identity and Islamic higher learning are prerequisites to social and political change.

The main objective of this book is developing a theory and a practice of educating Muslim woman outside the patriarchal discourse that views woman as the passive depositor of culture. I recognize the danger of using the category "Muslim woman," but my treatment of "gender" and of "Muslim" to change contemporary gendered global policy making justifies such usage. I discuss the pedagogical, historical, and theoretical issues of actualizing the Qur'anic educational principles of conscientious religio-moral rationality that Muslim women (or men) may use to affirm their identity and to self-identify with Islam's goal of justice. This goal requires direct access to and conscientious knowledge of the Qur'an, and autonomous action apart from any intermediary.

It should surprise no one, therefore, when I argue that the Qur'an is the root of democratic feminism in its broadest sense, a creative view of egalitarian active participation in the community's decision-making process. A woman who consciously chooses the Qur'anic worldview as her primary identification to achieve justice actually furthers this broad sense of democratic feminism. She effectively frees herself from the limitation of biological gender identification (which often relegates woman to the role only of wife or mother). Shifting from conventional discourses, including feminist discourses that try to free women from cultural constructions of gender, into the discourse of human moral and cognitive autonomy, may shed new light on understanding Muslim woman and her education and consequently help generate new readings of the Qur'an.

By starting with North America (the United States and Canada), the intention of this book is mainly to emphasize the core issues in educating the Muslim woman (and man), and their relevance to contemporary discussions of Islam, Muslim women, and Islamic education beyond the familiar geographical and cultural boundaries of the "Muslim world" and beyond the geopolitical boundaries of "global democracy." This temporal and spatial journey from North America to South Asia via the Middle East beginning in 1990s and moving back to circa 623 is intended to show the lack of effective development in Muslim female education and to reveal the persistent problem—the general lack of woman's self-identity and leadership initiative—and its implications for gender justice. This book is unique and of critical importance in the way it dissects (closely examines) unjust practices across cultures vis-à-vis the Qur'anic principles of justice and moral autonomy.

This book challenges readers in the fields of Islamic studies, Islamic and religious education, women's studies, area studies, global development studies, and Muslim women's studies to reexamine the established parameters and assumptions in these respective fields. It invites the reader to a much-needed dialogue on the prevailing views of Muslim women and of Islamic studies in general. By providing a different discourse regarding the role of women in cultural interaction and global affairs, this work also challenges policymakers to strive for a nonconfrontational understanding of the Islamic worldview. It suggests that by shifting the gendered discourse into the religio-moral rationality discourse this work will achieve this understanding and maintain enough tension to keep an equilibrium between the Islamic and America-European values while seeking global citizenship. This book is also intended as a primer for courses on Islam, Muslim women's studies, international and comparative education, and cultural studies and as a resource book for Muslim women around the world.

I would like to thank all the Muslim women who struggled with me through the last ten years of a participatory action research work. I also wish to thank the following for their interest and contributions to different aspects of this work during the research and development processes: my maternal uncle and constant intellectual resource, Zuhair Al Baba, and my first mentor in Islamic philosophy and ethics, the late ʿAdel AlʿAwwa, both professors at Damascus University; my closest family members and most arduous critics and supporters, Muawia (my husband) and Nobl Barazangi (my daughter and living proof of the possibility of upbringing within the Islamic worldview in Western societies); and Koko Elizabeth Bättig von Wittelsbach, Maysam al Faruqi, Rahel Hahn, Mohja Kahf, Sharifa Alkhateeb, Hanan Lahham, Jawdat Saʿid, Muhammad Shahrur, and Gisela Webb, whose intellectual and spiritual support cannot be expressed in words. Comments on different versions of this manuscript by the three official reviewers, including Charles Butterworth and two anonymous reviewers, were invaluable. Julie Copenhagen, Michael Engle, and Robert Kibbee at Cornell University Library went above and beyond the call of duty to support this work. Judy Healey's editing of the first version and Koko Elizabeth Bättig von Wittelsbach's editorial and intellectual suggestions on the second version were also invaluable. Muawia Barazangi, Rahel Hahn, and Gisela Webb brought added focus to this work as they read different parts of the final draft. My thanks to Amy Gorelick and Susan Albury, the University Press of Florida acquisitions editor and project editor respectively, are also in order. Without Amy's interest and support and without Susan's diligent and professional assistance in the editing process of the manuscript, this work would not have come to light.

Introduction

Woman's Identity and the Qur'an

During the past few years evidence has emerged that young Muslim female scholars and activists are increasingly using the two main sources of Islam, the Qur'an and the Hadith (the authentic tradition of the prophet Muhammad) in their daily lives. In America as well as in other Muslim societies, Muslim women are bringing positive change to the conception and practice of Islam. However, it would seem that most of these young women have not yet identified themselves with Islam; that is, they rely in their interpretations on traditional arguments about the Islamic texts, according to which oral or textual interpretations have authority on a par with the Qur'an itself. Consequently, these women are actually reinforcing conventional perceptions of Islam without introducing a new reading of the text in space and time, as the Qur'an directs all believers to do (Qur'an, 96:1, 3; 17:14, 71).

My book is the work of a Muslim woman attempting, as Frederick Denny (1989) describes Fazlur Rahman's work, to relate anew the Word of God to the world of the second quarter of the fifteenth century AH.[1] Although I agree with most of the scholarly work of Fazlur Rahman (*Islam and Modernity*, 1982; *Major Themes of the Qur'an*, 1980; *Islam*, 1966; *Islamic Methodology in History*, 1965 and 1995; and others), I take issue with some of his interpretations by presenting a pedagogical reading of the Qur'an (see chapter 2). I am also adding a new dimension to Rahman's reading and that of others. Denny (1989, 100) states that the "work of the Muslim intellectual, both in the sense of *'ibada* and *ijtihad* (an act of faith and of an intellectual discourse or individual reasoning), is composed equally and inseparably of both the *perceptive and the formulative intelligence*. Its greatest effort is relating anew the Word of God to the world in each generation." Because I speak as *murabbiyah* (an educator), I intend this book to affirm the self-identity of the Muslim woman as an autonomous spiritual and intellectual human being through Islamic higher learning, and I also intend to further the task of relating the dynamics of Qur'anic pedagogy—learning, knowing, teaching, and living Islam.

Islamic higher learning here means accessing the Qur'an and the entire range of early Qur'anic sciences that included what, in later historical contexts, was separated into *naqli* and *'aqli*. Since the human-endowed capacity to rationally internalize (*'aqli*) the textual meaning (*naqli*) is a prerequisite to making a conscious moral choice of the Qur'anic worldview, separating these two components resulted in a dual problem. First, Islamic higher learning did not fully take place among the subsequent generations of Muslims who did not receive the message directly from prophet Muhammah. Second, women were excluded from the entire process and, eventually, from either component of this higher learning, particularly the process of making meaning of the text. Thus, I pursue this project not only as *'ibada* and *ijtihad* but also from within the mandate to understand and to communicate the "gift" of the Qur'an pedagogically (Denny 1989, n32). A pedagogical reading of the Qur'an involves a process of making the learner aware of and able to theorize on Qur'anic principles and to distinguish these principles from a knowledge of the Qur'anic rules in order to facilitate interpretations and the conditions for their application (see chapter 5).

In earlier writings I have argued that Islamic higher learning is a human right and a responsibility for the Muslim woman. That is, a woman has a basic right to participate in the interpretation of the Islamic primary sources, the Qur'an and the prophetic tradition, in order to gain and claim her identity with Islam (Barazangi 2000, 1999a, 1997). Because my task could not be completed in the three decades I have spent deepening my understanding of reading the Qur'an ontologically (philosophy of value) and epistemologically (philosophy of knowledge), nor will it be completed in my lifetime, I regard this project as also a gift,[2] namely, the gift of dynamic learning and knowing Islam as a rational, living belief system.[3] Only through individual autonomous moral and cognitive integration and a sound leadership initiative can this belief system be made practicable.[4] I refuse to approach the learning and teaching of the Qur'an as a job to be "done" in a cursory manner or to "sacrifice myself for the survival of the species," as Arkoun (1994) suggests. I would also argue that because the thinking of women (or of men, for that matter) has not grown out of a mind-set of self-sacrifice for the sake of getting the job done, Qur'anic dynamics, especially in social fabrics involving gender, were rarely, if ever, realized among Muslims. Qur'anic dynamics require active participation, a participation that has been denied to women in general. Consequently, Qur'anic dynamics are not fully incorporated in societies that claim Islam as a way of life.

The purpose of this book is neither apologetic nor dogmatic moral coercion. Instead, I seek to regenerate the dynamic interrelation of the pedagogy (the arts of learning, knowing, and teaching), the epistemology, and the ontology of the Qur'an with those who have consciously chosen its worldview and attempt to live that worldview. Furthermore, this book intends to move the perception of Muslim woman from the ideal of the virginal, pious female, and from the reality of the follower with a proxy morality, that is, from an image relegated to and manipulated on the margins of Muslim societies, to that of the active agent, a believer who affects a change in history.[5]

My method is that of engaging in *ta'ammul* (reflective understanding) and *ta'amul* (action-oriented) learning with those who choose to take the same route toward the same goal, focusing in particular on certain Muslim interpretations concerning Islam and women.[6] My goal is to understand why these Muslim interpretations and intellectual discourses did not lead to completing the task of changing attitudes and policies concerning gender within the societies that call themselves Muslim. My pedagogical reading of the Qur'an, my method, and my curriculum explain why the woman's voice was not included in the early structure of Islamic religious knowledge even though, according to Leila Ahmed (1992, 72), some women contributed to the content of that knowledge. I would like to point out here that I am intentionally staying clear of the argument that patriarchy in the Arabian society or among Muslim males was behind gender injustice, not only because other historical evidence may prove otherwise, but mainly because I use gender neither as a unit of analysis nor as a premise for rereading the Qur'an.[7] Essentially I employ a pedagogy of religio-moral cognizance or rationality in order to explain, first, how individuals cannot change their views about the world and its structure without changing the structure of the context in which they live. Otherwise, they remain outside the existing structure, which will be maintained in its status quo. Second, with my approach I explain that the latter process is exactly what happened among Muslims when they, particularly the women, did not actually change their perception about the meaning of "*La 'ilah 'illa Allah,*" there is no god but God.[8] By accepting the authority of text interpreters as though their authority was as binding as the authority of the Qur'an itself, the practice of "*La 'ilah 'illa Allah*," the basic tenet of the affirmation of God's sovereignty, has veered away from its Qur'anic intention.

The Theme of the Book

Given that the majority of examples presented in this work are taken from among North America Muslim women, I start by explaining my theme in the context of the early American women's movement. I then present my arguments by moving between the early Muslim community in Arabia (ca. 632) and the contemporary Muslim community in North America as well as in Syria (the two places where I have done most of my empirical research).

Beth Waggenspack (1989, xiii) quotes Elizabeth Cady Stanton as saying "Self-development is a higher duty than self-sacrifice." In response to Stanton's argument I would contend that development of self is not only a higher duty than self-sacrifice but that self-development calls for and requires identification of self in order to be realized. In the following few paragraphs I want to examine the significance of Stanton's argument with reference to the Qur'an as the primary *living* text of Islam.

On the dedication page of volume 2 of Stanton's *The Woman's Bible* (1972 edition), Stanton writes: "Genesis Chapter I says Man & Woman were a simultaneous creation. Chapter II says Woman was an afterthought. Which is true?" Since others use Stanton's quote and identify her question "Which is true?" as central to their work (e.g., Matthew et al, 1998:8), I find it necessary to begin my pedagogical reading of the Qur'an with the story of Creation and its concomitant concept of *khilafah* (trusteeship, vicegerency) in the Qur'an.

The Creation story in the Qur'an, found in "Al-Nisa'" (The Women), 4:1, is presented as follows:

> O Humankind (*Ya'yuha al-nas*), be conscious of [or in equilibrium with] (*ittaqu*) your Guardian God (Allah), who created you *of a single* personal entity (*nafs wahidah*). Created, of the same entity, its [grammatical feminine gender] mate (*zawjaha*), and from them scattered abroad many men and women, and be in equilibrium with Allah by whom you are accountable to one another, and the wombs (*al-'arham*); surely Allah ever watches over you.

In quoting both Stanton in *The Woman's Bible* and the Qur'an, I continue one traditional intention and change another. That is to say, I continue in the intention of the Qur'an by reading it in space and time; I continue the traditional intentionality of my Muslim foremothers and fathers who saw the reading of the Qur'an as basic to practicing it; and in one way, I continue Stanton's tradition in that she sees the reading and rereading of the text as fundamental to changing the status of women who accept the Bible. At the same time and despite the acceptance of variant readings of the biblical story, I still depart from Stanton's apparent intention to incorporate women's perception by specifically calling it *The Women's Bible*. I also depart from the conventional Muslim readings and interpretations. That is, it is not my task or that of any other human being to edit the Qur'an, for it offers the Word of God as the source of value and knowledge to all believers. The fact that Qur'anic words are eternal and may not be changed or edited does not make them static in their intended meaning or place them in an absolute realm beyond reading in space and time. Rather, the words of the Qur'an should be read and constantly reread and reinterpreted in space and time. Without such engagement (rereadings and reinterpretations), humans may not be described as moral and rational beings who consciously identify with and directly access the Qur'an, and thus benefit from its guidance. This capacity for moral and rational derivation of a meaning from the eternal words and the immediate acting on the derived meaning to change one's behavior is what qualifies a human being as a Muslim by choice, that is, a self-identified Muslim. The Qur'anic emphasis on the human as being created of one single entity (*nafs wahidah*), as stated in verse 4:1, provides internal evidence for this argument. Had the prophet Muhammad and early Muslims solidified their beliefs and praxis into a normative standard, the Qur'an would not have come to life (Rahman 1995, 11).

Thus, the central question of my book is not "Which is true?" nor which view of women should be included. My central question rather is *"Who has the authority to reread and interpret the Qur'anic text and how is it to be done?"*

To avoid misunderstanding, let me explain again what I mean by intended tradition, self-identity, interpretation, and change.

I, and other Muslim women who identify themselves with the Qur'an, need not change the "intended tradition" of the Qur'n or be accounted of doing so that we will be viewed as active agents. Rather, what needs to change is first and foremost the widely held belief that only select elite males are authorized (males who bestow upon themselves the exclusive authority) to interpret the text. Thus, a fundamental task for believers is to reinterpret all the verses relevant to the topic of who has the authority to read and interpret the Qur'an. This is obviously a subject of another book, and yet it is at the crux of this book.[9]

It is not the "Islamicity" of a person and her faith that is being put to the test by the argument for self-identity and self-identification. Rather, what is being put to the test are the assumptions through which that person identifies with Islam as well as the manner in which she (or he) draws her (or his) rationales for everyday affairs directly from the Qur'an. In order to bring about such a change in assumptions, we need to address the historical development of Islamic thought and how Muslim males have arrived at the currently prevailing exclusionary conclusions.[10] I will discuss this historical development by addressing three fundamental issues: one, the story of Creation and the principle of trusteeship or vicegerency; two, female moral autonomy and the principle of modesty; and three, individual autonomous consciousness and its balance with social heteronymous action (socially imposed norms), while seeking equilibrium with Allah's guidance (*taqwa*), as discussed in reference to the verb "*ittaqu*" (in 4:1 of the Qur'an).[11]

By "interpretation" I do not mean to propose a conventional atomization of verses or chapters of the text of the Qur'an. Instead, I look at the Qur'an as a collective, cohesive guidance possessing its own system and providing a course of action (*minhaj/shariʿa*) for each individual to learn within a particular framework and to engage by acting on what one learns within that guidance. Note that the Arabic term *sharʿ* or *shariʿ* is often confused when making reference to what is known as "Islamic law." The constructs "Islamic law" and "*shariʿa* laws" do not represent the Qur'anic *Shariʿa* (with a capital *S*), meaning the collective guidelines of the Qur'an that encompass an intertwined moral and legal bind once the individual accepts the guidelines as his or her belief system, nor do they represent the Qur'an's principles. "Islamic law" or "*shariʿa* laws" (with lowercase *s*) are mainly used by Orientalists in reference to jurisprudence opinions, documented in books of *fiqh* (jurisprudence) and supported by some Qur'anic verses and Hadith narratives. By giving those opinions a legal character, known in the West as "law," Orientalists and most contemporary Muslims have confused the Qur'anic *Shariʿa* (guidelines) with other legislation or canonized laws.

Finally, by "change," I propose a transformation in history that changes presuppositions as well as social structures in order to mitigate historical stagnation. As the making and writing of history is a changing process, I aim at effecting change in both conceptions and attitudes concerning women and of women, and not merely a superficial change in individual behavior and organizational structure.

Therefore, and because of this latter reality, and given these prerequisites, that is, to live the intentionality of the Qur'an, the first chapter of this book addresses the conditions for reading pedagogically and the methods used in such reading. The second chapter addresses the story of Creation and trusteeship in order to set the groundwork for women's involvement in planning and executing the course of action in the *minhaj* to achieve *taqwa*. In the third chapter, I examine the issue of autonomous morality and modesty, especially in attire, since the polarized discourses about woman's dress have been the most troubling and most limiting to Muslim women in their endeavors. The purpose and intent of these discussions is to restore *taqwa* (equilibrium) as the measure by which the Qur'an distinguishes one individual from another and sets the standard by which to discuss whether or not an education can even be considered Islamic (chapter 4). Islamic education—or self-learning, according to the Islamic curricular framework that I propose—helps individuals to put into practice and exercise the role of the trustee (*khalifah*) by acquiring the capacity to balance individual autonomy and social hegemony or heteronomy within the natural and divine laws (chapter 5).

I conclude this work by explaining how the Muslim woman's self-identity and self-identification with the Qur'an may bring about and sustain fair changes both in the understanding of Muslim women and in their realities. My argument also clarifies that I do not concern myself with "Islamic feminism" as defined by Fernea (1998) and others, even though they attempt to address Muslim women's issues from the women's own perspectives. In the concluding chapter I discuss why both Muslim male interpretations and academic feminism have failed to account for Muslim woman's self-identity.

The Rationale for Reading the Qur'an Pedagogically

Several groundbreaking writings by Muslim women scholars in recent years have brought forward views of Muslim women that contradict the image of an oppressed cultural group or an oppressing patriarchal religion (e.g., Hassan 1982; Ahmed 1992; Wadud-Muhsin 1992 and Wadud 1999; and Webb 2000). These writings, significant as they may be, have not been able to change the generalized image of the "veiled women of the harem," an image that some Orientalists and Western media continue to promote.

Nor have these writings changed the image of the Muslim woman as dependent member in the Muslim social structure, an image that many Muslim apologists and followers of precedent (*muqallidun*) want us to maintain. The root of these images is to be found in the way in which the majority of Muslim women, including many intellectuals, have been taught to perceive women's role in society and in the religion. Changing these images, therefore, calls for a change in perceptions and realities that can take place only when Muslim women themselves change how they identify themselves with the Qur'an. I began my pedagogical reading of the Qur'an after exploring the process and history of education and educating in Islam, particularly with regard to Muslim women, and in response to the existing scholarship by and about women in Islam. It is a journey between polarized views about Muslim women in the past and present. As my research demonstrates, only a few Muslim women have been able to relate a basic knowledge of Islam to public affairs. By being excluded from participating in policy making (that is, the interpretation of the text) and from leadership positions, Muslim women have not been able to change perceptions and attitudes or their own realities. I have therefore concluded that without identifying themselves with the Qur'an, the self-realization of Muslim women may not take place.

In the West Islam is commonly viewed as a patriarchal religion incompatible with the Universal Declaration of Human Rights and, in particular, with the demands for women's rights.[12] Hence, my question: "How can the scholarship activism of self-identified Muslim women change current perceptions of Islam and women from North America to South Asia?" I argue first that women's involvement in decision making (that is, participating in the interpretation of the Qur'an as well as in discussing the human rights documents) is critically needed in many Muslim communities and societies, and second, self-identification with the Qur'an offers a way to eliminate the secondary status of women because it is based on defining the issues from *within*. Thus, identification with the Qur'an is, I would maintain, a prerequisite to defining the issues by and for Muslim women, and it is more likely to generate more substantive and lasting change than any other model. Third, I argue that the attempt to transplant Western secular systems of education and Western feminists' views into Muslim communities and societies through the academic institutionalization of the study of Muslim women ignores the spiritual and intellectual worldview of the people who identify with the Qur'an and will not lead to lasting "solutions" to the problem of the secondary status of women.

In contrast to those Muslim males who would often respond with an apologetic or confrontational approach to colonialism and imperialism, female scholar-activists who are self-identified Muslims have often opted for the Qur'anic stipulation to use religio-civil parameters for social change. These Muslim women (such as the American and Syrian grassroots groups with which I collaborate), and other Muslim women who embrace the Islamic worldview as central to their identity, could reverse the process of generating polarized images about Islam and Muslim women by critically examining and adapting human rights documents and by critiquing gendered interpretations and human rights violations internationally as well as locally. By reading the Qur'anic foundational principles pedagogically, and by interpreting from the place of that mandate the Universal Declaration of Human Rights, the United Nations General Assembly 1979 Convention on the Elimination of All Forms of Discrimination Against Women (CEDAW) (United Nations 1995, 1996), and U.S. and Canadian women's proposed amendments to their countries' constitutional mandates (e.g., Waggenspack 1989), these women scholar-activists may succeed in bringing back the mutual consultation process of *shura* among all Muslims, women and men. Furthermore, by discussing not only issues such as property ownership and inheritance, divorce and custody of children, and testimony and leadership in Islam but also issues of the autonomy of belief, freedom of expression, and public participation, they bring into the purview of Western "democratic" societies such as the United States, Canada, and others, the essence of Qur'anic justice, including Qur'anic gender justice.

This process is more critical than the mere establishment of equal rights or the democratic process of majority voting, because it calls for a partnership that involves all individuals in a community and is not limited to a few, namely the elite. This process also is more critical than the argument of Orientalists, such as Bernard Lewis (2001), merely to reform, liberate, or democratize Islam through changes in the status of women after the Western model. First, Lewis seems to apply Rosenthal's (1960, 2) understanding of the Hebrew meaning of *herut* (freedom, meaning submission to the law) to the understanding of the Arabic/Islamic meaning of free (*hurr*) or free will (*hurriyah*). In Islam, however, the order is exactly the opposite. Free will is a prerequisite to accepting, understanding, and employing the moral guidance of the message of the Qur'an, and this acceptance becomes legal and binding only after the individual makes the conscious choice to accept or reject the message, not because it represents the law. Second,

Western discourses, particularly feminism that relies on the politics of difference, as is the case in the nation-state civic democracy, often dismiss Muslim women's self-identity as "religious." Third, as will be discussed further, despite minor changes, the attitudes of the majority traditional male 'ulama (scholars of Islamic sciences) and policymakers have not changed. They still consider preserving customary traditions tantamount to preserving the Qur'an, the law, or the constitution. This is why some Muslim women, including some of my coresearchers, resist Western feminism and the nation-state form of democracy, as well as Muslim male elite conception and practice of the consultative process (shura)—wherein participation is limited to the select few, and women's participation is an "add-on" or serves only to address "women's" issues.

Given some similarities between Qur'anic principles and those proposed in human rights documents, we may further conclude that when self-identified Muslim women bring the above ideas into the purview of Muslim societies, more sustainable changes will be achieved for women in Muslim societies as well as for women in general. The data presented in this work will, among other things, also establish strong evidence to substantiate my argument that the history of early American suffragettes share common ground with that of contemporary Muslim women everywhere. In addition, data on early and recent historical events in Muslim societies in the East and the West indicate that Muslim women scholar-activists who identify themselves with the Qur'an can effect as much of a change in the struggle for human justice as in the struggle for women's rights and gender justice, particularly in the American experience.

That said, I would caution against the hasty assumption that mere inclusion of Muslim women as the subject of study in a new field of academic endeavor, such as the recently developed field of Middle East women's studies, can bring about the changes intended by the self-identified Muslim women. This inclusion may well co-opt such changes in present-day institutional structures. Neither would such changes yield a sustainable and just effect if a number of Muslim women were simply included in governing parliaments or consultation councils (majalis al-shura). Rather, the changes intended by the self-identified Muslim women require an understanding of the worldview of these Muslim women and of how their views differ from the views of Muslim feminists who are not self-identified Muslims or those who condone universal-solidarity approaches to social transformation without a specific and explicit ontological grounding and self-identity. Furthermore, such changes require that Muslim elites modify their views of women's trusteeship, morality, and authority to participate in the interpretation of Islamic texts.

Educational Discourse of Muslim Woman's Self-Identity: Did This Discourse Actually Occur?

Individual Muslim women and Muslim women's groups of different disciplines and backgrounds are increasingly seeking avenues of change that are closer to self-identification than feminism. The collection of essays published by Webb in 2000 may serve as a case in point. The essays in Webb's volume were conceived in 1995–96, and, interestingly enough, the "event that served as the final catalyst in the development of this volume was the enthusiastic audience response and near mandate to publish the papers delivered by the panel on 'Self-Identity of Muslim Women' at the 1995 Annual Middle East Studies Association (MESA) meeting" (Webb 2000, xiv).

By relating cultural studies to the rethinking of women's participation in and their interpretation of primary Islamic texts, some contributors to Webb's volume also took another step toward changing their position. For example, Mohja Kahf, a contributor to Webb's volume and a participant in the "Self-Identity of Muslim Women" panel, opened another window to understanding Arab Muslim women's literary work as significant "for modern Arabic cultural studies." In her pragmatic analysis of the memoirs of Huda Sha'rawi (1879–1947), Kahf not only rereads Huda's autobiography but also relates this work to the role Huda had in making a significant contribution to the course of events of her time (1998, 54).

Maysam al Faruqi, another contributor to Webb's volume and a participant in the "Self-Identity of Muslim Women" panel, added another perspective to the understanding of the study of Islam. Her two essays, "Self-Identity in the Qur'an and Islamic Law" (2000) and "From Orientalism to Islamic Studies" (1998), show the role that traditional Muslim interpretations and Western studies of Islam have played in creating misconceptions about Islam and Muslims, and emphasize the role and mandate that women have in rereading the Qur'an.

As a third contributor to Webb's volume and the organizer of the panel on self-identity, I captured this trend by tying the change in the image of Islam and Muslims in the United States to a change in the perception and the realities of Muslim women everywhere (Barazangi 1998a). In the editorial of the same publication, the 1998 special edition of *Religion and*

Education, I emphasized moral and intellectual autonomy of women as a prerequisite for Islamic education. In other works I drew a relationship between self-identity and democracy (1999a), and explained how women's higher Islamic learning is a prerequisite for their acquiring their human rights (1997, 2000).

Other Muslim women scholars have written about pioneering Muslim female figures of different eras and in different areas, and have emphasized the significance of Muslim women in history. Nevertheless, to my knowledge none have approached these figures from the angle of their pedagogical significance. Sonia Amin (1996, 8–10), for example, opens a fourth perspective to understanding Bengali Muslim women's pioneering educational and literary work in the same era as Huda Sha'rawi in writing about "the new woman in literature." Amin argues that the work of the women figures of the time, as exemplified in the work of Rokeya Sakhawat Hossein (1880–1932), is significant "for cultural studies of the new Muslim identity," but she chooses to address this historical significance by way of attributing the universalistic approach of Rokeya and her contemporaries to the secular trend of the time. While there might be truth in this, the fact that Rokeya and her other contemporaries were not part of the curriculum for the next generations of Muslims is not coincidental. Their omission indicates that some elements are missing in the reports on these scholars and their activism. Amin may have overlooked the possibility or misidentified the fact that Rokeya was identifying with the Islamic universal principle of egalitarianism, and that this principle was the actual driving force behind the conscientiousness of Rokeya's activism. Regardless of whether this was an oversight, and whatever the principles that might have informed Rokeya's intentional cognizant morality, the obscurity of Rokeya's and others' work for social change instigates my question concerning the pedagogical significance of these Muslim women.

Because of the historical interaction between the West and Islam, U.S. missionaries pioneered efforts toward modern education of Muslim girls (see, for example, Houghton 1877, and Jessup 1874) and have recently advocated women's rights in Muslim countries by supporting efforts to export "democratic principles" and "human rights values" to Muslim countries.[13] In this context, the question of exporting Western ideals is not the only one of special significance. Rather, the question that gains special significance concerns how Western women have borrowed and might be borrowing—knowingly or unknowingly—from the Qur'an the demands for voting, property ownership, name preservation after marriage, divorce and

custody rights, and other issues of gender justice. When traced on intellectual, philosophical, and pedagogical levels, the special significance of that
line of inquiry might reveal the importance of understanding Muslim
woman's potential contribution, or the lack thereof, to history.

Knowledge, Policy Making, and Leadership Initiative

Perhaps it was because of, or in spite of, these missing elements in reporting that Rokeya's and similar works were ignored by both Muslims and
Westerners or remained concealed and unexplored. Muslims did not want
to admit their malpractice of Islam (be it the extremists' attempt to prevent
women from learning how to read and write, or the *muqalliduns'* attempt
to prevent women from fully participating in the interpretation and understanding of Islamic texts); and Western colonialists, Orientalists, and
missionaries did not want Muslim women to be liberated from within the
Islamic worldview. Meanwhile, some of Islam's principles were borrowed
or translated into democratic principles and modern women's demands
while Islam was chastised as patriarchal and antithetical to democracy, human rights, and gender justice. To focus on the pedagogical significance of
Muslim women figures in history, therefore, means to construct a discourse for self-identity and identification with the Qur'an and with Islam
as a worldview and a culture regardless of geographic or ideological affiliation. The construction of this discourse aims at understanding the content
of and the assumptions that underlie the knowledge to which these pioneering women figures were or were not exposed. We need to answer
whether or not these women figures and their female contemporaries had
direct contact with Islam's primary sources. How did they interpret their
sources? They probably did have contact with primary sources, but what
other sources and interpretations did they rely on and draw from when
they constructed these individual and collective narratives of historical
events in Islam and within the given time and place of other histories?
Why is it that the significance of these Muslim women historical figures
remains anomalous and that their work did not translate into major social
and legal changes for Muslim societies as had been the case in Western
women's movements in less than a century? Or did these Western women
bring an actual substantial change in their societies?

I believe that the construction of a discourse from self-identity from
within Islamic reality will help in charting a course of knowledge and providing guidelines for changing the image and the reality of the Muslim

woman as well as the concept of Islam with which she identifies. Furthermore, it will help effect a fundamental change in the perception of Muslim women, namely, to change the mind-set operating with notions of second-class citizenry in order to embrace and practice the gift of autonomous human trusteeship as the Qur'an emphasizes in the second chapter (2:30). To chart these guidelines requires that each individual critically examine her own assumptions and their sources, hence the necessity to access the primary sources directly. To do so constitutes the first step toward self-identification with the Qur'an and with Islam. Historical documents tell us that this step was hardly taken by Muslim women. Is this indeed the case, and if so, why?

The relationship between knowledge and public policy has become so subtle that only a few scholars seem to have discussed it with regard to Muslims (e.g., Eickelman 1985) and to Muslim women (Barazangi 1982 through 2000). Yet this relationship is pertinent to the core issues of Muslim women and is essential whenever and wherever matters such as the mere right to literacy and schooling versus active participation in the interpretation of the Qur'an and modernity versus tradition are invoked. For example, in discussing Louis Dumont's (1986) notion that order in modern society is based on a complementary relationship between modern and premodern perceptions, George Stauth (1992, 4) asserts that this tense complementary relationship is present in the discourse of [Western] modernity and Islam. I would argue that this assumed complementary relationship has been expanded to include the postmodern issues of gender equality, and that most male scholars and religious leaders perceive and propagate the female's role as complementary to that of her male guardian. With the exception of the biological role of woman in reproduction and the caring for a child, the notion of a male-female complementarity in the sociopolitical order, while reflecting the views of many male Muslim scholars and leaders, actually contradicts the basic Qur'anic principle of human autonomous trusteeship in the natural order of justice and in mutual domestic consultation (Barazangi 1996, 80). The argument for complementarity also contradicts Webb's description that my "propaedeutic argument not simply for women's right to education but for the right of Muslim women to higher religious education (active participation in the ongoing 'reading' and interpreting of the Qur'an) as the foundational means to becoming the spiritually and intellectually autonomous person mandated in the Qur'anic view of the individual, male or female, as 'trustee' of God" (Webb 2000, xvi).

In addition to the tension between ideals and practice in Muslim societies and communities, the institutionalization of complementarity in terms of sociopolitical order has brought about a movement away from the pedagogical dynamics of the Qur'an and of Islamic jurisprudence into a single, codified, fixed law, called Islamic law or *shari'a* (Barazangi 1997, 48–54). Among Muslim thinkers and in Muslim polity, the tension between the modern and the premodern has resulted in a dichotomy and separation between "modern" and "traditional" perceptions. Consequently, the social sphere has become like that of the European social order of the time: public versus private. Similarly, the educational system was separated and dichotomized into "secular Western" versus "religious Muslim," and female and male educations were separated and became different from each other (Barazangi 1995a, 406). The dichotomization and ensuing separation within Muslim education have also resulted in the alienation of Muslim woman from her self-identity as mandated in and through the Qur'anic view of the individual. Muslim women experience the effects of this separation and frequently find themselves concretely no longer understanding the basis for the traditional while being unfamiliar with the modern.[14] Consequently, the grounding needed for affirming her identity and for bringing up the ensuing generations of girls and boys has been destabilized for the Muslim woman (Barazangi 1998b, 8).

The Evolution of the Book

It was partly because the majority of Muslim women scholar-activists, both inside and outside of North America, refused to adhere to the image of the "oppressed," to the Western model of "progress" and modernity, or to Muslim males' model of exclusivist authoritarianism that the attitude in parts of the academic community began to change during the mid-1980s. A few academics began to see valid research possibilities in the issues arising from the presence of Muslim woman in Western and other academic institutions as well as from her presence in the streets with her "different" garb. Examples range from discussions on women in Islam (Hassan 1982) to the search for Islamic feminism (Alkhateeb, al-Hibri, and Wadud in Fernea 1998). Yet, to the best of my knowledge, no source, Muslim or otherwise, discussed woman's self-identity with the Qur'an and how that question is related to her being educated in Islamic sciences so that she can interpret Islamic texts and literature, thus determining her own liberation and boundaries.[15] Although we begin to see a glimpse of such discussions in *Qur'an and Woman* (Wadud-Muhsin 1992), in Hassan's feminist theology (1991), and—on the level of grassroots activism—in the founding of Muslim women's national organizations such as the North American Council for Muslim Women (NACMW) led by Sharifa Alkhateeb and aimed at raising women's consciousness,[16] the drive toward Qur'anically grounded self-identity was not fully articulated until the theme was discussed in the "Self-Identity of Muslim Women" panel. The self-identity project was paralleled, on a policy-making level, by the founding of the Muslim Women's Georgetown Study Project (MWGSP), which was led by Maysam al Faruqi and produced a special version of the United Nations document, CEDAW (UN, 1996), from the perspective of Islamic jurisprudence.[17] NACMW and MWGSP, as well as the grassroots women's group in Damascus, Syria, were important platforms for developing the self-identity project. By contributing to the discussion of a platform from the Islamic perspective prior to the Beijing 1995 Fourth World Conference on Women and to other relevant forums, the self-identity discourse was also tested pedagogically before it was intellectually theorized. This book will show how this movement toward a Qur'nically grounded self-identified Muslim woman has called and continues to call for the restoration of Qur'anic dynamics and the pedagogical reading of the Qur'anic text and related sources.

It is worth noting here that although I consider valid Hassan's (1991) argument for the need of a feminist theology as a means for her liberation, my argument for Muslim women's higher Islamic learning and self-identity is not intended for the development of feminist jurisprudence (*fiqh*), or contemporary *fiqh* in general. Instead, I am mainly concerned with Muslim women's own restoration of *living the Qur'anic dynamics*— that is, the Qur'an's gift and mandate to be read, reinterpreted, and reflected upon—without which Muslims cannot ground their claims for justice or claim to identity with Islam. If this restoration were to result in the development of a sound feminist *fiqh*, it would compound the value of this book, but given the scope of my work, it can only represent a secondary goal here.

For centuries Muslim women have been the objects of discussion conducted almost exclusively from outside of Islam and have been viewed as a single category or a homogenized group. Moreover, few resources have been used for educating Muslim girls beyond mastering literacy or mastering home economics skills, and even fewer writings have been devoted to the broader and deeper issues of Muslim women's education.[18] My active engagement through a participatory action research approach with Muslim women's Islamic higher learning is a means to enable and equip myself and these women coresearchers to understand and to practice collaboratively an individual intention to accept Islam as a belief system and a worldview (as presented in the Qur'an and extrapolated in Hadith), and is not intended as a dogmatic imitation of the documented Sunnah (traditions of the Prophet) nor as a theological system of *fiqh* and law books. Fazlur Rahman (1995, 14) asserts that the "necessary instrument whereby the prophetic model was progressively developed into a definite and specific code of human behavior by the early generations of Muslims was responsible personal free-thought activity." I would further contend that to rely solely on others' interpretations of Islam's primary sources is by itself evidence that the Muslim woman's right to identify with the Qur'an and to act on her acceptance of a Qur'anically grounded Islam is being significantly compromised.

My pedagogical interpretation of the Qur'an and its primary principles of Islam is justified by the empirical evidence from my work with American and Syrian Muslim women who, despite their scholarship-activism, have not yet engaged to a large extent with this responsible personal free thought. The further synthesis of historical and contemporary documents concerning gender justice offers further evidence that such documents become rather helpless in the face of the rigid reasoning one can encounter in Muslim communities. Fazlur Rahman (1995, 15) elaborates: "This rational thinking, called '*Ra'y*' or 'personal considered opinion,' produced an immense wealth of legal, religious and moral ideas during the first century and a half [of the Islamic era] approximately." Although contemporary Muslims are producing an almost similar number of legal, religious, and moral ideas, the outcome shows not only such great divergence on every issue of details that it becomes chaotic; more importantly, it could hardly be claimed to be the result of the kind of free rational thinking that Rahman postulates. One could detect, the plethora of legal, religious, and moral ideas not withstanding, an inability to depart from the interpretations of others and a lack of exercising *ijtihad*, including exploration and designation of new methods and discourses, for such a practice of *ijtihad* would certainly go beyond relying on the already existing "sunnah" of the preceding community.[19] I would therefore like to emphasize that I am not interested in a fifteenth-century AH (twenty-first century AD) wave of "Ra'y" similar to that of the wave in the second century AH (seventh century AD) when Muslim intellectuals and leaders turned from individual free thought and gave way to "the systematic reasoning [*qiyas*] on the already existing *Sunnah* and on the Qur'an," as Rahman describes it, instead of taking the advice of Ibn al-Muqaffa' (d. AH 140) to exercise their own *ijtihad*.

Thus the purpose of this book and its preceding research is not only to speak in a Muslim feminine/feminist voice but to create a new venue for exploring and engaging the sources of Islamic education and Islamic higher learning within the framework of the Qur'anic mandate and call to self-identity. I will present three decades of examining and learning from the worldview of Islam and its dynamic to bring about change and to act as a social transformative power within the realities of nearly three centuries of "educational reform" in the majority Muslim societies. My criteria for evaluating these "reforms" are not merely oriented at the question of the place women occupy in the Qur'an (the ideal), but how early Muslim women like 'A'isha and Hafsa, wives of the Prophet, and Fatima, the Prophet's daughter (ca. 623) identified with the Qur'anic revolution. I will explain the significance of these women's pedagogy by examining how they responded to their contemporary social structure in light of their understanding of Islam and what we can glean from it.

The discourse of self-identity with the Qur'an brought forward the discussion of the experience of these early Muslim women ('A'isha Bint Abi Bakr, Hafsa Bint 'Umar, and Fatima Bint Muhammad). Their presence in the public arena is indisputable. What is of interest here, and of possible dispute, is the question of how these women identified with the Qur'an and with Islam. I answer this question by addressing how they transformed themselves and their surroundings (whether they actually did that) and whether they deciphered the signs of the Qur'an, as Rahman (1982) suggests all Muslims be able to do and as I recommend as the first step toward self-identification. Whether or not these women fully deciphered and practiced the signs of the Qur'an and understood their pedagogical significance could help us answer the question whether it is plausible to translate Islamic theory of moral and cognitive autonomy into a pedagogical and ethical dynamics within any social context. It must be left up to the reader to draw such a conclusion.

The Thematic Structure of the Book

The thematic structure of the book follows from three main areas of inquiry: (i) the relation of Qur'anic pedagogy to sociopolitical order, (ii) the interaction between the world of learning and that of public policy making, and (iii) the effect of the perception of these early Muslim women on the thinking and reality of contemporary Muslim women. A set of questions is addressed in each of these areas.

First, were early Muslim women figures, like ʿAʾisha, Hafsa, and Fatima, successful in relating Qurʾanic pedagogy to the sociopolitical order of their time? If so, then how and why, and if not, why not. After all, one could argue that being the wives of the prophet Muhammad and the daughters of the first two caliphs, Abu Bakr and ʿUmar respectively, ʿAʾisha and Hafsa may have had a certain "image" and held special privileges. Furthermore, being the daughter of the Prophet and married to her father's cousin ʿAli, also an early Muslim companion to her father and the fourth caliph, Fatima may have had a similar "image" and enjoyed similar privileges. I am, in this context, mostly interested in understanding how their insights did or did not contribute to the formulation of an Islamic discourse of self-identity that has implications for the present perception of women and their status. Both ʿAʾisha and Hafsa, especially ʿAʾisha, have become well-known authorities in recounting the official history of Islam (Ahmed 1986, 671), yet we hardly see any report of their involvement in the interpretation of the history that they transmitted (nor even the hadith they are reported to have narrated) for public policy (Spellberg 1994, 3). Only in recent books do we see Muslims, especially the Shiʿa, read back in Islamic history in order to make a special place for Fatima beyond that of being the mother of Hasan and especially the martyr Hussein, who died in a battle between two Muslim political rivals.[20] Can this lack of place, attention, and involvement be ascribed to the fact that most of the history was written by men and written more than one hundred years after the death of these early female figures of Islam? Or could its roots lie in the possibility that these women did not actually identify with the Qurʾan in the sense described earlier? Do we have reason to believe that the "first woman" of Islam, as Ahmad (1986) would like to present ʿAʾisha, and her contemporaries were involved but that their involvement was obscured? Synthesizing the resources available to Ahmad and to others from within the point of view of self-identity will further help explain this view as well as set the tone for both the methodology of this work and for the criteria by which we can assess Muslim women's pedagogical significance, or the lack thereof, for a just Islamic discourse.

Second, how has the interaction between the world of learning and that of public affairs affected the perception of Muslim women's issues and their solutions across history? Why were matters of social justice in modern Muslim societies focused only on women's morality as represented in their attire, while matters of economic justice and class justice so often denied to them—for example, inheritance, the right to property, and their participation in policy making—were ignored? What have been the implications of this interaction between knowledge and public affairs in international and national policy making, especially as far as the policy making of the technologically modern world vis-à-vis the Muslim world is concerned? How has the tension between the Muslim modernists' approach vis-à-vis the Western approach to modernity affected the transformation of the discourse of knowledge and sociopolitical order? How did the interfacing of social order and restrictions on individual morality come about, particularly among women in contemporary Muslim societies? Why did the Qur'anic *mandate* for individual morality become obfuscated and ultimately ideologized into the heteronomous morality following the introduction of Western secular schooling and missionary education?

Third, how has the predominant perception of Muslim women as being "controlled" by Islam affected their thinking, their perception, and their realities as both individuals and as a group that represents one-tenth of the world population living in the so-called open global society of the twenty-first century? How have postmodern Western views on social order (e.g., Habermas 1979) affected the pendulous relation between "order" and "hegemony"? Do recent readings of the Qur'an concerning the role of women (e.g., Webb 2000; Shahrur 2000 and 1990; Wadud-Muhsin 1992, and Wadud 1999; Mernissi 1993 and 1992; 'Abd al-Rahman 1987 and 1968a; Rahman 1996 and 1966) bring "Islamic" and "Western" views closer together or further apart? Do the views presented in such readings reflect something larger than women's issues or will they further emphasize gendered policies?

I analyze the Islamic goal of *taqwa* in order to make apparent what is missing in the education of the Muslim woman. My research, represented in the chapters of this book, discusses key elements that are missing, missing even from the curriculum of contemporary Muslim schools in North America as well as from feminist, development, and universalist theories and practices of social change. Each chapter redefines the problem from within the framework of identification with the Qur'an by integrating Islamic educational views. It would, no doubt, seem easier if I were to present the status of Muslim women and their identity and then discuss issues of education. The entire theme of this volume, however, is built on the

Qur'an's emphasis on the all-pervading relation between Islamic identity and the conscious (self-reflective) cognition (*tafakkur*) of the Qur'an.

I define education as a conscious process of conceptual and attitudinal change. Since this change requires and presupposes the individual's identification with a worldview, to analyze each element separately and only within historical and contemporary feminist or Muslim contexts would not suffice. Only when the woman (and the man) gains autonomy in the Qur'anic sense, namely, by understanding the Islamic belief system without depending on intermediary secondary sources and identifications, then and only then can we claim to have achieved Islamic education. The Muslim woman's ability to achieve such an autonomous intellectual and spiritual state is the first step toward a constructive, meaningful pedagogical reading of the Qur'an, hence, toward Islamic learning, knowing, and teaching, and, consequently, toward *living Islam* and gender justice.

A brief note on the English transliteration and translation of Arabic/ Islamic words and Qur'anic verses is in order here. To maintain a consistent transliteration, I primarily follow the *International Journal of Middle East Studies* (IJMES) system with some modifications, using diacritical marks only for ayn (') and hamza ('). Proper names and quoted words were kept as published by the cited authors or transliterated by the Library of Congress. The translation of the Qur'an is either taken directly from or modified on the basis of Abdullah Yusuf Ali (1946), Arberry (1955), or Asad (1980). The variations in these translations support my argument that English and other translations are in part responsible for the confusion of meanings in contemporary interpretations. One only needs to read the different English meanings given to the word *zinah* (translated variously as ornaments, beauty, glitter, and beautiful apparel), for example, to understand the concern.

Pedagogical Reading of the Qur'an

This book suggests forging new ground for the Muslim woman who consciously identifies with the Islamic worldview of *Tawhid*—the belief that there is no deity but God (Allah, in Arabic). This worldview is not intended to think only of God, but to think also of humans as equal before God who is the source of value and knowledge. The goal of this worldview is to deconstruct human hierarchy and balance natural and social laws, that is, *taqwa*. To execute identification within this worldview, some Muslim women, including myself, have been engaged in rereading and reinterpreting the Qur'an.

To extract a legal ruling or to extrapolate a meaning for day-to-day practice, Muslims typically reference four traditional types of Islamic texts: the Qur'an (the primary source for the ideals), the Hadith (the primary source for the prophet Muhammad's extrapolation and practice of the Qur'anic guidance, also known as the Sunnah of the Prophet), the *tafasir* (the major commentaries or exegeses on Qur'anic text), and the books of *fiqh* (the collections of major jurisprudential interpretations of the Qur'an and jurisprudential rulings based on the Hadith, mistakenly known as Islamic law or *shari'a*). The last two sources, the *tafasir* and the books of *fiqh*, are secondary to the Qur'an and Hadith. Although we find a few women narrators of the Hadith (mostly on the authority of the Prophet's wife, 'A'isha), there is hardly any female name associated with the commentaries or the jurisprudence texts. Whether this was the actual practice, or whether the widely circulated history books simply did not document the whole story is the subject of another part of my research and another book.

I focus mainly on the Qur'an because it is the divine text of Islam and because the results of my scholarly activist work suggest that the central issue for Muslim women is their lack of participation in the interpretation of the Qur'an. Rahman (1995, v) states that conventional readings of the Qur'an usually follow the widely used principles of Islamic thinking—the Qur'an, the Sunnah, *ijtihad*, and *ijma'* (consensus of the scholars or the community). Even when some readings follow these traditional principles, interpreters differ in the way they combine and apply them. The differences, Rahman argues, "can cause all the distance that exists between stagnation and movement, between progress and petrifaction." Rahman emphasizes that "these four principles are not just principles of Islamic jurisprudence but of all Islamic thought," and he explains how the different applications of the four principles have evolved during the first two centuries of the Hijra years (marking the Muslims' migration from Makka [Mecca] to Madina [Medina]), highlighting the enriching dimensions of the dynamic and lively application of these principles, and describing how the solidification in the application of these principles resulted in stagnation.

Mir (1986, 1), on the other hand, distinguishes four historical types of combinations and applications of these principles:

1. The *traditionalist* exegesis is based on *ahadith* (pl. of hadith) or Sunnah, occasions of revelation, and historical reports or opinions of early authorities. Two widely used commentaries of this type are by al-Tabari (d. AH 311/AD 923) and al-Suyuti (d. AH 911/AD 1505).[1]

2. The *theological* exegesis seeks to defend and support particular theological views against rival views. The prime example is al-Razi (d. AH 606/AD 1012).

3. *Literary-philological* exegesis concentrates on the rhetorical, linguistic, and grammatical aspects of the Qur'an. Its best representation is found in al-Zamakhshari (d. AH 538/AD 1144).

4. The *juristic* exegesis deals primarily with the Qur'anic verses containing legal injunctions, and presents the views held by their schools on these verses. Early works of this sort are those of the Hanafi jurist al-Jassas (d. AH 370/AD 980) and the Maliki jurist, Ibn al-'Arabi (d. AH 543/AD 1148).

What concerns us here is the absence of Muslim women from this field, namely, that of reading Islamic texts and developing exegeses. Even more poignant is the absence of women from reading and interpreting the Qur'anic text, particularly for pedagogical and ethical meanings. I am not talking about recitation, but about intended, direct reading to derive meanings and draw rational judgment, or what Rhaman calls "personal considered opinion." With the exception of the Egyptian writer ʿAʾisha ʿAbd al-Rahman's (1968a) literary reading, and the "process-oriented reading" of the American scholar Amina Wadud-Muhsin (1992), I am not aware of any comprehensive reading of the Qurʾan by women. Of course, there are numerous scattered articles, essays, or even recent monographs that present theological, jurisprudent, or historical interpretation of specific Qurʾanic texts within a larger discussion of women-related issues.[2] The most recent and notable of such works is the essay written by Maysam al Faruqi, titled "Self-Identity in the Qurʾan and Islamic Law" (2000).

Al Faruqi distinguishes between the Qurʾanic text and the derived Islamic law, explaining how outsiders and the male jurists have *diverted* (my emphasis) from the Qurʾan's internal rules of interpretation, leading to unjust and unjustified extrapolations of meanings concerning basic issues for women. Thus, the focus of my pedagogical reading of the Qurʾan is intended to emphasize the need for female involvement in a similar comprehensive treatment of the Qurʾanic text from within its own rules of interpretation. This is what I intended when I initiated the project and the ensuing panel, "Self-Identity of Muslim Women," in 1995. The self-identified Muslim woman (or man) is the Muslim who recaptures the meaning and the practice of being a Muslim by choice; who intimately accesses (without any intermediary), consciously understands, and rationally interprets the Qurʾanic text using its own rules. As is found in the Qurʾan, "God has revealed the most beautiful message in the form of a Book, consistent with itself" (39:23).

My participatory action research work, reported in part in this book, is not designed simply to promote the Muslim woman's right to education. It also promotes her right to Islamic higher learning (mistakenly coined as "religious education" or "religious learning"). What I mean by this term is a deeper knowledge of the Islamic primary text, the Qurʾan, that will eventually change her own perception of self as a Muslim, not only the customary attitudes about the role of women, but subsequently the conventional reading and extrapolation of meanings from the Qurʾan. Al Faruqi asserts, "Muslims take Islam to be the first source of identity, not an additional ideological superstructure" (M. al Faruqi 2000, 74). By realizing this meaning of identity and reference, a Muslim (man or woman) will subsequently realize his or her humanity as a trustee of God on earth (*khalifah*), and the meaning of *taqwa*, the standards by which he or she are judged and differentiated. *Taqwa* (from Arabic) denotes the ability to balance individual autonomous reasoning with social hegemony and the natural divine laws.

I argue that Muslim women's active participation in rereading the Qur'an is the foundation to becoming the spiritual and intellectual person (the Muslim person) mandated in the Qur'anic view of the individual as trustee or vicegerent. I also argue that the absence of women from earlier Qur'anic readings is at the root of the misreading of the meaning of Islamic identity and trusteeship, interpreting the principle of *khilafah* stated in the Qur'an—"God said to the angels: I will create a trustee on earth, and God taught Adam the names of all things" (2:30–31)—as if it were limited solely to the male's political and theological leadership, and as if "Adam" were limited to the male human. By this misinterpretation, Muslims also confused human leadership with God's Lordship. Thus, reading and interpretation of a woman who is self-identified Muslim is the only course of action for a change from these conventional readings.

It is important that Muslim women themselves interpret the text fairly and without presenting their own biases, whether their biases are based on gender, race, or class. Hence, the need to develop a list of checks and balances for women's pedagogical and ethical interpretation becomes eminent. Given that the Qur'an provides such a list, partially discussed in the "Text and Meaning" section of this chapter, it will be up to the reader to follow those points of checks and balances. In the rest of this chapter, I discuss the goal of this pedagogical reading of the Qur'an, the relationship of text and meaning. I then describe the sources and challenges and define the problem, the argument, and the evidence that call for the self-identity model and the pedagogical reading of the Qur'an.

The Goal

The goal of my work and of this book is to stimulate discussion about the Qur'an, in the community as a whole, not only among women and for women's issues. Women's participation in the interpretation of the text is not a modern innovation. The Qur'an states: "God created the pairs (*al-zawjayn*)—males and females" (53:45). Similarly, verse 4:1 states: "O humankind (*ya'ayuha al-nas*), be conscientious of [or in equilibrium with] your Guardian God (*Rabbakum*) who created you of a single [personal] entity (*nafs wahidah*). Created, of the same entity, its [grammatical feminine gender] mate (*zawjaha*)." Thus, woman is not a secondary principle of human creation but is a primary principle in the human pair. Therefore, women's reading and interpreting the text is long overdue and is a necessary condition for their humanity and for their trusteeship, ensuring the application of both the mandates and the gift of the Qur'an as well as the success of women and their community.

Although Muslim women in North America have begun changing attitudes and traditions, they have not yet acquired the same status as their male counterparts, mainly because, with the exception of a few women, they have not yet taken the initiative to exercise leadership in departing from the traditional applications of the four principles of Islamic thought. Muslim women are also gaining recognition in the American landscape of "religiosity," and one might even claim that American Muslims have been better recognized in American society generally because of the women's work, as explained below. But even these American Muslim women have not yet achieved what women from other religious traditions have: being recognized as religious authorities in theory and in practice. The Islamic Society of North America, for example, the largest and one of the oldest Muslim organizations in America, and its affiliate, the Association of Muslim Social Scientists, were in the year 2000 still scrambling to include women on the electoral ballot of their boards.[3]

Muslims often emphasize that the Qur'an views the family as the primary unit in socioeconomic affairs and whenever women's issues are discussed. Yet when the issue becomes that of women's participation in policy making and leadership in the interpretation of Qur'anic text, the majority ignore the fact that the creation, as stated in the Qur'an, 4:1 and 53:45, was that of the personal entity and from it its mate—the male-female pair. Instead of realizing the individual right and responsibility as a rational, legal entity within the Qur'an—human trusteeship as being equally mandated for the male and the female—Muslims often extend the male's economic responsibility toward the female, as stated in the Qur'an, 4:24, to the female's individual intellectual and spiritual right and responsibility. Al Faruqi explains the distinction in the meaning of the verse when translating or interpreting the Arabic word "*bima*" as "with what" instead of as "because" (M. al Faruqi 2000, 83). When the meaning of the verse is extended to intellectual and spiritual rights, generalizing the causal relation between economic responsibility and moral authority, Muslims not only deprive females of their legal self-identity and worth within Islam, but they also deprive the Muslim family and community from the benefits that such responsible free-thinking females present. For instance, although the number of Muslim women scholar-activists is increasing in major American universities and other institutions, and their contribution to the public-policy process has been more visible and is often more effective than that of their male counterparts (see the contributors to the 1998 volume of *Religion and Education*), only some Muslim communities are awakening to such contributions and are cultivating their benefits.[4]

Furthermore, no community has come to realize that these contributions are the result of women's autonomous understanding of the Qur'an and not merely due to these females' pious character or self-sacrifice. An individual may neither internalize nor practice Islam fully unless she (or he) is a Muslim by choice. Therefore, any interpretation that does not formulate the meaning of a text from the (rational) Islamic perspective is simply irrelevant in the decisions that affect that individual's belief and life. Al Faruqi emphasizes that the starting point is in—and only in—the system of beliefs about the world and about self that the individual willingly and rationally chooses (M. al Faruqi 2000, 74).

Text and Meaning

In this section, I briefly identify the common rules that define the Islamic faith and the methodology of its interpretation to which most Muslims subscribe, at least in theory. The shortcomings of some of the historical derivations in combining and applying these rules call for the women's urgent involvement in, and the creation of a new reading of the text. We see the basis of this new reading being laid down in the volume *Windows of Faith* (Webb 2000), but the comprehensive work of rereading the Qur'an is in the making. I hope that this book and the project of self-identity will be recognized as part of this rereading. The five most basic rules of interpretation, and the rules that I follow, are the following:

First, the Qur'anic text is God's Word and hence these eternal words cannot be constrained by time, space, or any interpretation that is given to them. What has happened is that Muslims, perhaps unknowingly, were constraining these words by their interpretations, particularly after approximately the first century and a half (Rahman 1995, 15).

Second, Islam, as *Din* (worldview), is basically textual, not based on an event (as, for example, Christ's resurrection in Christianity). The *content of the text* is what defines all Islamic beliefs, from the divine authorship to the relation of God with humanity. Al Faruqi reminds us that it is not because of the prophet Muhammad that Muslims accept the Qur'an;

rather it is because of the Qur'an that they accept the authority of the Prophet (M. al Faruqi 2000, 76). What happened is that Muslims, to a large extent, reversed the order when they idealized the Prophet and his extrapolation on the Qur'an, his Sunnah. Most contemporary Muslims even forget that the Prophet's extrapolation (resulting in external texts to the Qur'an, the Hadith) does not supersede the Qur'anic text. Even while recognizing the organic connection between the ideal and its practice (the Qur'an and the Sunnah), knowing that the Qur'an is its own best interpreter should be a good reminder to Muslims—including women—that they need not be rigid in applying these interpretations and practices literally. It is not merely the participation of women in the reading and the interpretation of the text that is at issue here, but it is their self-identification with the Qur'an and with Islam as the *Din* of *Tawhid* that is of utmost concern. *Tawhid*, as was discussed earlier, means that the authority lies only with God, whose guidance is in the text of the Qur'an.

Third, the order of the Qur'an was established by the Prophet on divine inspiration, not on the Prophet's personal extrapolation, and according to aesthetic, not thematic or chronological rules (M. al Faruqi 2000, 89). Thus, chronological orders of revelation suggested by concordances of the Qur'an are external to Qur'anic content and may or may not be binding if the interpretation based on them does not follow the lexical and linguistic rules of the Qur'an and if it does not consider other related verses within the particular chapter and among the 114 chapters of the Qur'an. Islamic law derives its legal authority from the Qur'anic text itself, not from a scholarly or juristic determination, nor from an institution, such as a mosque, a state government, or a court (M. al Faruqi 2000, 77).

Fourth, the first revealed verses of the Qur'an, that is, verses 96:1–2, call for reading in the name of God, emphasizing the divine origin of the text and of creation from a clot. These verses and verses 3–5 remind humans about the transcendence of God as the ultimate teacher who created humankind (Adam) as a moral being to act on his or her own choice to carry or to refuse the trust by his or her rational ability to read the text and write the meaning. Thus, a woman's absence from participating in reading and interpreting will only contradict these verses and the mandate of 39:23 that the Qur'an be consistent with itself. The individual woman who follows conventional readings blindly ends up neither reading the text nor realizing the ultimate authority of God, nor participating in interpreting the Qur'an from within. Eventually she loses her morally enjoined responsibility of reading that enables her to make an informed choice and a legally mandated interpretation. Even jurists who claim that they are following the rules of interpretation end up doing injustice when they claim authority over the woman by virtue of their interpretation. Whether it is the absence of women from reading the text or an interpretation of the text from outside the Qur'an, the result is the same—the intent of the text is altered.

Fifth, by definition, the legal interpretation of the Qur'an is based on the whole text and must take all its content into consideration. The occasion and the context of revelation are to be taken into account, too, but because they have been historically derived, they are not binding. Hence, an interpretation corroborated by the verses of the Qur'an is stronger than an interpretation corroborated by these externally derived sources (M. al Faruqi, ibid.). Historically, Muslim male interpreters emphasized these latter occasions and the narratives associated with them as the source and the evidence in making a ruling or a judgment, ignoring the basic source, the Qur'an itself. Injustice was thus committed twice, toward the text and its rules of interpretation, and toward the intended Qur'anic content as superseding any historical source, including the prophetic extrapolation.

The Sources and the Challenges

Traditional Qur'anic commentaries, the prophetic Sunnah, and the work of jurists (known in the canonical books of *tafsir*, hadith, and *fiqh*, respectively) represent a base in my assessment of the state of affairs. I argue that these canonical works have, perhaps unknowingly, separated the perceptive from the formulative intelligence of the Qur'an. I explain the influence and the long-lasting effect of this separation by analyzing, first, the pedagogical significance of three representative women of early Islam as narrated in these canonical books, and second, the most recent readings of the Qur'an by both males and females. Although I keep all of these sources in their right place as secondary to the Qur'an, I focus on the recent readings because they have presented, in the last forty years approximately, somewhat different interpretations of the Qur'an and of Islam from that of the conventional Orientalist (the Western scholar's view of Islamic studies), the *'alim* (the traditional Muslim religious scholar), or the apologist (the scholar who uncritically adopts modernized interpretations, mixing assumptions and methodologies).

Recent works by Muslim scholars are different from the traditional canonical books, not only because of their methodology and focus in their reading of Qur'anic and Islamic meanings, but also because of their purported explicit reading of the Qur'an's favorable stance toward human rationality and the dignity of the "person." Standing out among these works are Malik Bennabi's scientific reading, Fazlur Rahman's thematic reading, Jawdat Sa'id's philosophical reading,[5] 'A'isha 'Abd al-Rahman's literary reading, Mohammed Arkoun's anthropological historicity, Amina Wadud-Muhsin's hermeneutic reading, and Muhammad Shahrur's linguistic reading.[6] My basic question with regard to all these landmark works is how to implement their different readings pedagogically so as to apply the many significant insights contained in the readings in a way that will actually change the conception and practice of social fabrics involving gender in societies that claim Islam as their guidance. Reinstating the female in her primordial role, as opposed to the complementary role that is propagated in these societies, requires our analysis of the pedagogical significance (or lack thereof) of these works as well as the significance of the three women figures from early Islam, that is, 'A'isha, Hafsa, and Fatima.

For example, although Arkoun differentiates between Qur'anic fact and Islamic fact, or Qur'anic epistemology and Islamic theology (1994, 3), he stops short of explaining the pedagogical differences in relating Qur'anic epistemology vis-à-vis Islamic theology. He alludes to the historical differences between the two when he discusses the "right of the mind to truth" or reason, stating, "For a Muslim the struggle for this right always takes place within dogmatic closure. I recall in this respect the fight of philosophers to loosen the hold of the theologian-jurists on the exercise of reason. Ultimately, orthodoxy overcame the 'rational sciences,' which it termed intrusive (dakhila)" (93). Yet, Arkoun also points out the central difficulty of the human and social sciences: "Out of concern for objectivity, a scholar declines to intervene as a person" (ibid.). But, in my view, the intervention of the "person" in the position of knowing is affected by the person's values, and perhaps emotions, regardless how objective she or he may claim to be. What is of concern in Arkoun's differentiation between theology and epistemology is not the missing element of "reason" in the first, but the lack of showing how "reason" and "value" integrate while the "person" is actively aiming at knowing the Qur'an. Unless we assume that a belief in a worldview stems only from reason, meaning that a nonbeliever could read and explain religious texts and reach the same conclusions as those of the believer, Arkoun needs to readdress this matter and clarify his differentiation.

I am approaching this task—of the pedagogical reading of the Qur'an—by coming to the Qur'an "prepared to receive its commands and, in the process, to be inspired by its light" (Qur'an, 42:52). For my moral conscientiousness to approximate the religio-moral identity itself, I exercise my reason to understand the above-cited works (Bennabi, Rahman, Sa'id, 'Abd al-Rahman, and so on) and to bring forward a different understanding from the one that caused Islam to be transformed into what Rahman calls the "externality" interpretation (of the Qur'an), which became orthodox.[7] I am looking into these works in search of their effect on changing the social fabrics involving gender while the majority of the contemporary generation is reading the Qur'an either theologically or with the "enlightenment reasoning," as Arkoun rightly states. In other words, I am reinterpreting the Word of God for the new generation by explaining my experience and, to a certain extent, that of Muslim women who share the self-identity view, while reading the Qur'an and then evaluating these works accordingly.

Since both readings (the theological and the "enlightened reasoning") proved problematic not only epistemologically but also by not delivering a comprehensive change in the social fabrics, we are challenged to explain why these readings did not result in social change for women. As the new generation has not been able yet to either adopt or to be significantly affected by those cited works (Bennabi, Rahman, Sa'id, 'Abd al-Rahman, and so on), I extend the following explanation by Arkoun to my specific concerns with woman's morality. He states that the theological reading has fixed the Orientalist image of Islam in a monolithic perception and practice, adding, "Europeans tend to reaffirm the untouchability and universality of their [the enlightenment reasoning] model" (1994, 4). He further states that even when Europeans speak of the enlightenment model's weaknesses, they demand that Muslim arguments be more "objective" and less engaged in recurrent forms of protest against the West and its model. I add to Arkoun's argument the following. First, the theological reading has also fixed the Orientalist image of the Muslim woman as the secluded dependent, the 'awrah, while the enlightenment reasoning tends to open the harem doors for outside ideas regardless of their validity for the society. The result is the dichotomy between the public and private, and between complementarity and autonomy. Second, I wonder if this assessment (of the theological and the enlightened reasoning of Islam) is behind the impression that the new generation of Muslims has "no way out." Is it because the new generation has not yet become aware of the significance of the recent works? Or is this generation incapable of understanding and, consequently, of applying the recent works and their insights to their own lives? I suggest the latter, as Arkoun himself attests: "As conceived and written, this book may present another difficulty that deserves clarification. . . . Even an enlightened public may find it difficult to fill the blanks left by illusive references to events and ideas I take to be generally known" (1994, 3).

The challenge before me in this book is, therefore, twofold. I first need to determine whether or not the new generation would benefit, and in what way, from the recent works, including my present work. To accomplish this task, I reflect with the new generation on their attempt to create new meanings. Just as Rahman analyzed the customary and traditional interpretations and practices of early Muslims,[8] to synthesize these attempts is to make explicit the problems and the solutions in any reading wherein pedagogical dynamics of the Qur'an are missing. Rahman explains the confusion between the Sunnah of the Prophet and the sunnah of the community of the time. I will analyze the new generation's confusion of religion (the practice of rituals and rules of "do's" and "do not's") and Islam as a worldview, both to complement his work and, most importantly, to benefit the community of our time. My analysis does not follow a chronological order, nor does it necessarily cover in detail all of the resources cited above (a task that is beyond my present goal). Rather, as I examine the current pedagogical credibility of all the major meanings generated by these sources, I need to move back and forth in time and among the works of each scholar or historical figure under consideration.

The Problem, the Argument, and the Evidence

In this section, I define the problem, present my argument, and outline the evidence for the need for a pedagogical reading of the Qur'an.

The Problem

In addition to injustices to women and to the text of the Qur'an discussed earlier, further injustices lie in the malpractice of the first revealed verses of the Qur'an that call for reading ("*Iqra*'") in the name of God (Qur'an, 96:1–2). Muslim women's participation in this reading is not an option, but a condition for being a Muslim. As this participation has been overlooked by Muslim societies, the lack of reading and interpreting of the text by women from within the text has resulted in three additional shortcomings: exclusion, prevention, and deprivation.

First, exclusion of women from involvement in their community's mutual consultation process, contrary to what the Qur'an dictates in 42:38, was based on the wrong assumption that women do not constitute a theological authority.

Second, the exclusion also prevented the woman whose affairs were being discussed from being a Muslim by choice, and from acting as an autonomóus human trustee who is also enjoined to act in equilibrium.

Third, the exclusion also deprived communities from applying God's justice and transcendence as the ultimate teacher and judge. "Blessed is God whose hand is the sovereignty, . . . who created life and death to try you, which of you is best in conduct" (Qur'an, 67:1–2), and not to "try" by gender, class, or race.

Since the above means of achieving *taqwa* never materialized in these communities, the challenge for my coresearchers and me lies not only in the issues we address or the approach we follow, but also in the source that we all use, namely, the content of the Qur'an and the principles by which some interpreters claim to abide. There are several readings of the Qur'anic text and corresponding definitions of the Islamic "self," but the primary definition of identity belongs to the domain of the Qur'anic law. The Qur'an limits itself to explaining the given meaning of the legal verses when a Muslim accepts the absolute unity of God and the truth of the Qur'an as divine revelation. Each Muslim must uphold, and is subject to, the legal and religious injunctions of the Qur'an as the basic infrastructure. By differentiating between the Qur'anic legal construct of the text and the legally derived construct (M. al Faruqi 2000, 78), a Muslim who identifies with Islam realizes that he or she could be subject to the law as stated explicitly in the Qur'an, not the law that was derived on the basis of the four principles—the Qur'an, Sunnah, *ijtihad,* and *ijma'.* Not being a participant in this latter process of derivation is the reason behind women's being short-changed and the unjust extrapolations of the meaning of the Qur'anic principles of *shura, khilafah,* and so on.

As some American Muslim women scholar-activists are claiming this participation, evident early on by their involvement in interfaith dialogues, they are also upholding the legal and religious injunctions of the Qur'an. When the officers of the Muslim Student Association of Columbia University opposed my making a presentation about Muslim women in 1967 at the religious activity building, Earl Hall, their opposition was based on the assumption that the Qur'an should not be read outside the institution of the mosque. Therefore, I was not only able to present a different perspective on women's issues from the dominating view of the time, but I also reintroduced the Qur'anic concept of interfaith interaction—"Say to the People of the Book, come to a common ground between you and us, that we worship none but God" (3:64)—by asserting that the concern of these students had no basis in the Qur'an.

Incidentally, other women were—both now (see the names of contributors to *Windows of Faith*) and at the time—taking similar steps, but generally keeping (or being kept at) a low profile. Muslim women community leaders in the 1970s and 1980s, like Sharifa Alkhateeb in Philadelphia and Washington, D.C., Khadija Haffajee in Ottawa, Riffat Hassan in Kentucky, Zeba Siddiqui in Colorado, and the late Lamya Ibsen al Faruqi in Syracuse and Philadelphia, are only a few examples. By speaking up, despite the negative images of Muslim women and low expectations of them, these women were able to shake the conventional ground on which the Islamic tradition was being read. As I look back for a reflective evaluation, I still feel that the Muslim community at large has not fully awakened to this process that Muslim women are bringing forward. This is happening because Muslims have not fully realized that the authority of Islam lies in the Qur'anic text and not in its interpreters. This is why the road is still ahead for women to carry this task forth, and to strengthen and spread the changes that are taking place without allowing them to petrify into another stagnating period.

The Argument

I argue that Muslims throughout the centuries have oppressed women by stripping them—perhaps unintentionally—of their self-identity with Islam. By assuming that a woman's religio-moral rationality (*Din*) is the responsibility of her male household, Muslim communities not only denied women the Qur'anic meaning of *Din* but also violated the very first principle of Islam, the Oneness of the Deity, as the source of value and knowledge. In addition, and because of these assumptions, Muslims built the early structure of Islamic life without including the woman's voice either pedagogically or in policy making, affecting both the construction of "Islamic" knowledge and that of social fabrics and norms. Beginning with the construction of the Qur'anic sciences—the actual processes of interpreting the Qur'anic text (*tafsir*)—and ending with the mutual consultation and consensus of the community (*ijma'*), the woman's voice was, to a large degree, absent. This absence during the critical development of the structure of Islamic thinking and the Muslim community resulted in women's becoming followers of interpretations imposed by others and, consequently, relating to the next generations only through these interpretations. Unable to relate directly to the moral conscience of the Qur'an, their relating to the next generation was therefore void of the original message of the Qur'an as the moral guide (Barazangi 1997). Eventually, this inability led to women's participation in their own oppression.

Gradually, even marginal involvement of some women was made even less important by secluding them during the Friday congregational prayer—a gathering intended to deal with community affairs—and eventually from public life (Barazangi 1996). The net effect has been that the woman's capacity for exercising her religio-moral responsibility in the social balance has faded in practice to the point that it also faded from the conscious of both men and women, and also from their consciousness of the Qur'an. Being the condition for identifying with Islam, this lack of conscientiousness resulted in women's identity becoming defined by the collective image either of the secluded woman of the harem, or the temptress of the public domain. The effect of the Oriental image of the harem, for example, is no more harmful than the image of the tempting woman that the Mufti of Damascus in 1995 claimed during a Friday sermon in the Umayyad Mosque. Using a questionable hadith about Muslim woman's lack of modesty and her punishment in hell, he ascribed temptation (*fitna*) to the female as her natural disposition!

The Evidence

Contrary to the Qur'anic verse "and no [personal entity] shall carry the burden of another," repeated in 6:164, 17:15, 35:18, 39:7, and 53:38, the woman was made to carry the burden of the sin for the first fall, and eventually was to become dependent morally and socially and a burden religiously. Consequently, Muslim societies lost the ability to recognize that this basic shift from the Qur'anic view—and not the lack of practicing rituals or a form of dress for women, as generally preached—was the main reason for the deterioration of civility in public life. That is, as the woman lost her ability to pedagogically communicate the dynamics of Qur'anic morality, the next generations also started losing the Qur'anic message, and moved further away from the meaning of the Qur'anic message of

Tawhid. Since one cannot give what one does not possess, and by being considered as a burden, the woman's conscientious choice became, instead, the inevitable fate of being born a dependent female.

A woman with this secondary identification by her gender and with a proxy religio-morality could only passively transmit a message that had been polluted with the layers of interpretations she passively received. Thus, Muslim societies, particularly their intellectuals, may have related the words of the Qur'an through the religio-moral exhortation intellectually, theologically, and legally, but they have failed to relate the perceptive conscientious of the Qur'an. Throughout this book I visit three issues that I see both as evidence for my argument and as contributors to the present, negative state of affairs in the Muslim woman's learning, knowing, teaching, and living Islam. These issues are intertwined in their meanings, in their pedagogical dynamics, and in their implications. They are the story of Creation and vicegerency; the autonomous morality and modesty; and *taqwa,* or the equilibrated balance of individual conscientious moral choice and social action. For clarity, each issue is addressed in a separate chapter (chapters 2–4). In chapter 2 I examine the Creation story and its relation to understanding (i) the Islamic religio-moral-rational worldview (*Din*) as the framework for learning, knowing, teaching, and living Islam; and (ii) the problem of Muslims' idealizing human persons, and its implication for the perception of women's state of affairs.

The Religio-Moral-Rational Characteristics of the Qur'an and the Story of Creation

Rahman argues that the task of the Qur'an changed from the time the Meccan verses were given to the time of the Medinese verses. He wrote: "From the thud and impulse of purely moral and religious exhortation, the Qur'an had passed to the construction of an actual social fabric" (1966, 30). I contend that an actual change in the social fabrics involving gender was never constructed, even in the early period of Islam.[1] I attribute this lack of change partly to the fact that the Muslim woman did not take a leadership initiative in the moral-religious construction of knowledge to begin with, or was not given what Rahman calls "a fully-pledged personality." With the exception of a few incidents,[2] the Muslim woman did not identify with Islam as an autonomous moral being; she was neither prepared to know Islam as a rational belief system, nor prepared to receive Qur'anic commands directly and autonomously. Therefore, instead of following the Qur'anic mandates by working together as mates (*azwaj*) in order to construct an actual gender justice, the Muslim woman merely followed the traditional role of a female subordinate to her male household.

The majority of history books tell us that 'A'isha (the wife of the Prophet) merely narrated the Sunnah and, in later times, was sent back along with the other wives of the Prophet behind the *hijab*, the curtain.[3] By practicing the social customs as solidified by the "orthodox" interpretations, her public appearance was considered a negative act, especially after she became one of the leaders who fought in a battle after the assassination of 'Uthman, the third caliph. Although the mandates of the Qur'an dictate the religio-moral-rational personality for each individual as a trustee (Qur'an, 2:30), as an equal in the order of creation (Qur'an, 4:1; 7:189; 31:28; 39:6; 53:45; and so on), and as a partner in community affairs ("And every soul comes with a drive and as a witness," Qur'an, 50:21), the meanings of these mandates were not pedagogically applied, nor socially practiced as such, because the majority of women were not part of the movement from the Meccan psychological exhortation to the Medinese active construction of the social fabrics involving gender. So, for example, even when 'A'isha and the other wives of the Prophet were reported to argue with him concerning domestic affairs, none of them was named by the Prophet, or later on by the consultative community, as a public figure, a caliph or otherwise. Consequently, the construction of gender justice in the social fabrics was never completed because the voices of these women were not heard in public. Why?

Muslims marginalized the woman's role in the interpretation and communication of the message, and in the social balance, when they adopted the traditional biblical interpretation that Eve was created from "Adam's rib," ascribing maleness to the primordial human creation, Adam.[4] Contrary to the Qur'anic assertion that God created the pair/mates (azwaj) as male and female (53:45) from the same personal entity, and then from them spread a multitude of men and women (4:1), Muslims still use the Judeo-Christian tradition to translate and interpret these verses. Women were stripped of their role as trustees despite the Qur'anic chapter "Al-Nisa'" (The Women) that opens with the verse: "O humankind (ya'ayuha al-nas), be conscientious of [or in equilibrium with] your Guardian God (Rabbakum) who created you of a single [personal] entity. Created, of the same entity, its [grammatical feminine gender] mate (zawjaha)."

As a result, the Muslim woman herself was not allowed to take the leadership initiative to interpret the Word of God with the gift of coming "to the Qur'an prepared to receive its commands and, in the process, to be inspired by its light," as Rahman states, quoting the Qur'an (42:52). Instead, it was assumed that she could follow the interpretations of her male members of the household and other male elites, and continue with her task without seeing the light of the Qur'an in her own consciousness, or the light of the world with her own eyes. This latter issue is represented in today's stigmatization of the hijab, the segregating curtain or the form of dress vis-à-vis the meaning of Islamic modest dress, and its effect on the moral-cognizant development of women (discussed in more detail in chapter 3).

Evidence of women's surrendering the leadership initiative can also be found in what has been recorded about early Muslim women, including the role of the most exalted Muslim women, who are often reported in connection with their male progeny. Even those related to the prophet

Muhammad, such as 'A'isha and Hafsa (two of his wives) and Fatima (his daughter), were recorded in history in relation to the manhood of Muhammad and his prophecy, as preservers of his Sunnah. In searching through Ibn Sa'd's *Kitab al-Tabaqat al-Kabir* (1904), for example, we find two dominant themes projecting the image of these women. First, all the narratives speak of the women, including the Prophet's wives, as being given, or asked for, in marriage through their fathers or other male relatives, even after the Qur'anic revelation. Second, most of what was narrated about these women concerned their marriages, their giving birth, and their deaths. When an exception was made, narratives affirm that the women in question were not directly involved in the construction of Islamic knowledge. A striking example is found in the narrative in which 'A'isha was advised by Ibn 'Abbas (a companion of the Prophet) that she could receive Hasan and Hussein, the sons of Fatima, because they were in the class of *muhram*s (that is, not of the marriage category, being the grandchildren of the Prophet) (Ibn Sa'd 1904, 8:50). This implies that 'A'isha was neither allowed to make, nor was capable of making, such a deduction! The tasks of these women were restricted to comforting, reporting, and emulating; they did not participate in the interpretation of the Qur'an, nor were they participants in the historical making of the Sunnah of the Prophet, or the sunnah of the community.[5] They were not among those to whom Anas bin Malik, the great theologian of Medina who started serving the Prophet at the age of ten, attributes the consensus of opinion (*ijma' bi al-ra'y*).[6] Although these women were idealized from the early making of Islamic history, they did not fully participate either in making that history or in the construction (recording) of that history.

After discussing the problem of idealizing, I will discuss the Creation story and its relation to understanding the principle of vicegerency/trusteeship (*khilafah*). Then, I will relate the issue of Creation to the other two issues: the autonomous morality and the principle of modesty (chapter 3), and the balance of individual conscientiousness with social action, *taqwa* (chapter 4).

The Problem of Idealizing

Islam is neither an ideology that requires the ideal person, nor a fixed teaching that needs an authority figure.[7] The fact that the Qur'an only mentions two women—Maryam (Mary) and the wife of a pharaoh who in post-Qur'anic sources is referred to as "Asiya"—does not mean that these two women were active models, despite the fact that they were considered as spiritual examples. According to the reports, they did not take a leadership initiative in the knowledge generation process; they were content with being known as the silent pious, the pure, the virgin, and so on.[8] Nor can these women be considered as the ideal for a Muslim woman (or a man for that matter). Spellberg (1994, 152) suggests that the "critical notion of preference associated with Mary alone provides the most consistent precedent for the linkage of Khadija, Fatima and ʿAʾisha with a Qurʾanic archetype." I argue that Maryam, Asiya, and other women mentioned in the Qurʾan without names (Wadud [1999, 106] lists them) should be viewed as merely examples (*mathala/amthal*). We need to view these women just as *mathala*, as Abraham, Moses, Jesus, and Muhammad are viewed in the Qurʾan: "And Allah cites an example for those who believe, the wife of the Pharo . . . and Maryam" (66:11–12), and not as ideals or as archetypes.

To make a static, ideal model of any human figure, even the prophets, is against the core principle of Islam, *Tawhid*. Although Spellberg's intent might be to show the existence of a positive female example to combat the stereotyping of Muslim women in the negative, she apparently has missed the implication of such idealization on this principle. We will see later how far-reaching the implication of overlooking this principle is, by Muslims and non-Muslims, with regard to Maryam as an archetype of the Muslim woman.[9]

Similarly, and in a different context, Arkoun tries to deconstruct this static model in his criticism of both Muslims and Orientalists. Nevertheless, he overlooks this fact, as he asks, "How many women have mastered the biological, anthropological, historical, and sociocultural genesis of the condition of women in order to lead the battle for emancipation at the appropriate levels and in the interest of promoting the human being?" My response is that these women did not master any of these disciplines precisely because they have been sacrificing "their self-realization as *persons* (Arkoun's emphasis) so as to assure the survival of the species," as Arkoun expects from them (1994, 62). We find this concept of self-sacrifice dominating Muslim and non-Muslim males' expectation of females, not only in Arkoun's quote above; women themselves began believing in it to the point that they failed to realize their self-development.[10] My contemporary women scholar-activists and coresearchers are an example of how women are attempting to gain their self-identity, but their work, and mine so far, has not generated the pedagogical dynamics necessary to move beyond setting the example. These women could lose their leadership initiative by not maintaining active participation in generating both a new word and a new world with each new generation, instead of just helping to biologically reproduce the bodies of these generations.[11] These women need not repeat what generations of Muslim males have been doing: reiterating and commenting on the knowledge produced by their ancestors.

I contend that the ideal principles for a Muslim woman in the Qur'an are the same as those for a man (Barazangi, Zaman, and Afzal 1996), and that these principles do not need an archetypal female or archetypal male in order to be applied. I further argue that this search for the ideal in the person of another human is exactly what resulted in the failure of Muslims—intellectuals and laypeople alike, males and females—to realize the meaning of a "religio-moral-rational personality" as the core concept in formulating Muslim woman's (and man's) morality in line with the principle of *Tawhid*. Not realizing this meaning in the pedagogy of the Qur'an, Muslims accordingly failed to transform the social fabrics involving gender because, simply put, the woman was not involved in the interpretation process. Therefore, Arkoun's suggestion that Muslims avoided applying the new rules of Islam, such as those on inheritance, for fear of losing their patriarchal power status, can serve the purpose of this book better if it is understood in the context of the following historical incident. Ibn Sa'd (1904, 8:18) reports the story of Abu Bakr (the first caliph) refusing to give Fatima her share of her father's estate, basing his judgment on the following narrative that is attributed to the Prophet: "We [prophets] do not have heirs, what we leave is a charity." This story is a good example of the exclusion of women from leadership and knowledge construction. How else can we explain the fact that the Prophet has made a statement of such magnitude without informing his immediate family, especially his wives and his daughter? This is because inheritance for the female was one of the major changes in the Qur'anic gender revolution. As I am more inclined to interpret this particular narrative in reference to leadership inheritance (monarchy)—given the hadith context and given that the Prophet was using the occasion to abolish such practice in line with Qur'anic dictum, I am equally concerned about the apparent fact that the female members of the Prophet's household were not informed of such an important ruling, assuming that the narrative is accurate.

Whatever the explanation might be, Muslims failed to make significant changes in the social fabrics involving gender because they were looking for a precedent ideal after the death of the Prophet, or even at the time when the Qur'an was enjoining them to cut themselves off from prior practices (Qur'an, 2:170; 5:104; 7:28; and so on). Muslims in effect have moved from the text (the declarative knowledge of the principles) into policy (generating legal enactment of the principles) without giving credence to the importance of developing the Qur'anic pedagogical dynamics perceptually away from prior gender conceptions and practices. For example, when the Qur'an models the prophets Muhammad and Abraham as the "*uswah hasana*" (33:21), it does so to emphasize Muhammad's and Abraham's ability to separate their opinion from that of the revelation, as 'A'isha 'Abd al-Rahman (1968b, 4–5) asserts when discussing how people before Islam confused prior conceptions of gods, making idols of the messengers (*rusul*). By recognizing their humanness they affirmed that they did not want to be exalted as the Deity. It is equally ironic, however, that even when 'Abd al-Rahman herself quotes the Qur'an—"Say, that I am only a human like you, it is revealed to me that your God is Only One" (41:6)—to emphasize Muhammad's [and Abraham's] ability to construct this "new knowledge," she does not apply the same explanation when talking about Maryam and 'Asiya or women's equality in the context of the Islamic concept of woman's liberation (1967, 10). Why is it when the Qur'an models Maryam and 'Asiya as *mathala*, also quoted by 'Abd al-Rahman, the interpretations always follow the line of these women being the model of the idealized believers who obey the faith and submit to its interpretations through the existing social norms? It is perplexing how Abd al-Rahman acknowledges these women as examples (*mathala*), recognizing them as autonomous humans (1967, 9–10), talks about Islam freeing humans from being enslaved by other humans (1968b, 4), and yet continues to exalt Muslim woman's endowed acceptance of the "natural right of the man to have *qawamah* (superiority or guardianship) over her" (1967, 12). Despite her recognizing the meaning of their humanness and the fact that they were also entrusted with the message of the Oneness of God, as the Qur'an asserts (33:21; 60:46), not viewing Maryam and 'Asiya as *uswah hasana*, instead of seeing them as the exalted archetypes, is, in my opinion, the main reason behind such discrepancy in 'Abd al-Rahman's (and others') interpretations (see further discussion of *qawamah* in chapter 4).

Overlooking the Qur'anic perceptual pedagogy of "a fully-pledged religio-moral-rational personality" with reference to women is also evidenced in the writings of contemporary Muslim intellectuals, including Fazlur Rahman himself, whose interpretation of some aspects of the story of human creation I find troubling. His interpretation is troubling precisely because it may represent the same kind of gender bias found among earlier interpreters despite his gifted insights about the Qur'an. Pedagogically speaking, as new generations only work with interpretations instead of starting with the Qur'an itself, and by reading the works of Rahman and others as the new archetypes, they will miss the process of perceptual understanding of the Qur'an. In other words, they will follow predecessors' interpretations, and will consequently reinforce old attitudes with the new readings of the Qur'an.

The issue here is to understand the meaning of "Adam," the first creation of the human kind in twos/pairs/mates (male and female) who would carry God's trust (Qur'an, 2:30–35). Although we are told in the Qur'an that Adam was also a prophet (3:33), the rest of the Qur'anic verses speak of Adam as the symbol of the human creation.[12] These verses emphasize humans as being different from any other creatures by virtue of their ability to reason and to forget: "And verily we made a covenant of old with Adam, but Adam forgot, and we found no constancy" (Qur'an, 20:115), even when Adam received the perfect message of revelation. Bennabi (1968, 208–9) discusses this important process when explaining the difference between the prophet Muhammad's rationality (ra'y) and the reasoning of the Qur'an, quoting the latter: "And hasten not [O' Muhammad] in the Qur'an, ere its revelation hath been perfected unto you, and say 'My God! Increase my knowledge'" (20:114). By relating the meanings of the above two verses, 114 and 115 of chapter 20, it would become clear whom Adam symbolizes.

The Story of Creation and Vicegerency

If we accept verse 4:1—"O' humankind (Ya'yuha al-nas), be conscientious of [or in equilibrium with] (ittaqu) your Guardian God (Allah), who created you of a single [personal] entity (nafs wahidah). Created, of the same entity, its [grammatical feminine gender] mate (zawjaha), and from them scattered abroad many men and women, and be of equilibrium with Allah by whom you are accountable to one another, and the wombs (al-'arham); surely Allah ever watches over you"—as relevant to understanding the Islamic stance on women, a Muslim woman who identifies with the Qur'an becomes an essential partner in the interpretation process of the Qur'an, just as her access and participation in the interpretation process is a must for her self-identity. That is because human nature is distinguished by its nafs (Rahman 1980, 17). In Islam, there is no separation between mental and physical being, and *nafs* implies the totality of the person or the close relation between human heart and mind that realizes the existence of God through its relation with itself and nature. The compelling richness of these meanings in the Qur'an, 'A'isha 'Abd al-Rahman (1987, 34) wrote, is what allowed generations of Muslims to find yet new interpretations. Nevertheless, once a non-Qur'anic framework of interpretation was introduced or a particular interpretation was enforced as the ultimate one, both the richness and the ability of Muslim individuals to realize their direct relation to these meanings were lost ('Abd al-Rahman 1968a, 1:18). One sees, for example, how al-Ghazali's acceptance of the Greek, Christian, and Hindu concept of separating human nature into the mental and the physical created a dichotomy in Muslims' separating knowledge of the divine vis-à-vis the mundane, as affirmed by Rahman (1980, 17). Another example is how the concept of Adam and Eve from the Judeo-Christian tradition has influenced the prevailing translations of the above Qur'anic verse, 4:1. The feminine marking of the word *nafs* was changed to imply both sexes and translated into "person" ('Ali 1946). The feminine pronoun attached to *"zawjaha"* (her mate) was changed to a masculine pronoun and translated "his mate," and eventually the order of creation was reversed to imply that Eve was created of "Adam's rib" (Smith and Haddad 1982), despite the fact that the concept of Eve does not exist in the Qur'an. It is also true that the concept of absolute transcendence has profound implications for one's understanding of both divinity and human dignity. That is, each individual needs to be informed within his or her own capacity and language—"On no personal entity/soul (*nafs*) doth God place a burden greater than it could bear" (Qur'an, 2:286), and understand before he or she can practice Islam (Barazangi 1997, 51–54).

The meaning of conscious choice to carry the message of the Qur'an also became corrupted by the Muslims' adoption of the biblical interpretation of carrying the message as the burden of human sin. Muslims' adoption of this meaning that ascribes the "burden of Adam's fall to Eve" not only violates the basic Islamic principle that no one carries the burden of the other, but also has created a view in which the highest level of religiosity and religious knowledge is reserved for male priests or clergy. Consequently, male's protection against female's temptation (*fitna*) has dominated the public versus private relations and the power structure of knowledge. For example, as we will see in the next chapter, the concept of Islamic modesty was emphasized as particular to the woman, and her seclusion and segregation—socially and intellectually—became the means to curb her temptation, creating not only separate worlds of males and females, but also separate worldviews. Hence, the message of the Qur'an was reduced to a mere book that is inherited or passed from one man to another.

I therefore reiterate my earlier question: how is it possible for a Muslim society to provide the individual an autonomous, independent moral and rational entity when almost one-half of the society, the women, are paralyzed or not actively participating in realizing the Qur'anic meaning and guidance? Because Islam is affirmed to be both a belief and a social structure that is not based on submission but on action (Garaudy 1983, 179), being a Muslim requires active participation and not mere acceptance of teachings. By the same measure, how can we assume that the Muslim woman has regained her human rights without her direct involvement in the interpretation and implementation of the platform for action? History indicates that she was stripped of these rights many times under the guise of Muslim laws, of state sovereignty, or of the many standards in interpreting human rights. The strategy, therefore, is that she herself generates the meaning within the framework of self-identity with the Qur'an while maintaining the core concepts of Islam, and that we recognize that meaning as the operating principle for action (Barazangi 1997, 52). Hence, the state of affairs of the Muslim woman is not merely what we have been reading about in the last two hundred years—the problems of polygyny, divorce, child custody, and so on—but it is the lack of self-identity with the Qur'an.

Even as Rahman (1966, 38) asserts that the Qur'an has "immensely improved the status of the woman in several directions . . . the most basic is the fact that the woman was given a fully-pledged personality," he seems to emphasize the primordial status of the male figure. By limiting the translation of sulalah in the verse "We have created human beings (al-'insan) from a sequence of processes (sulalah) of wet earth" (Qur'an, 23:12) to mean the male reproductive semen in the equation of the human creation (Rahman 1980, 17), his translation could cause gender injustice even when he might not have intended it to do so. That is, it seems as if Rahman is contradicting his own argument about the "fully-pledged personality" of a woman because, even when we read, "God who has perfected everything God created, and began the creation of al-'insan from clay, and then made the human progeny from a sequence of processes (sulalah) of a despised water" (Qur'an, 32:7–8), we should not be limiting the meaning of ma' mahin, "despised water," to be merely the male semen. We would also be contradicting the Qur'anic assertions of (i) the creation of male and female, "We created you of a male and a female" (4:1; 7:189; 23:14; 30:21; 39:6; 49:13); (ii) creation of everything in twos (*azwaj*) (life and death, sky and earth, day and night, male and female); and (iii) reverence of the wombs after reverencing God (4:1). Finally, we would be missing the meaning of creation from a clot: "then, we placed the human in a drop (of seed, egg) in a safe place. Then we fashioned the egg into a clot, then the clot into a little lump, then into bones, then clothed the bones with flesh, and then produced it as another creation" (23:12, 13–14). In addition, we know that the woman also produces a nocturnal sexual discharge (*ma'*, water) that is also reported in al-Bukhari (1997, 1:171–72, hadith 280).

Furthermore, perhaps unintentionally, Rahman contradicts his earlier explanation of the trust, the relationship between God and human, and between the task and the gift, and of humankind as the intellectual, moral being—whereas each individual human has the right to, and is responsible to understand in order to execute the trust.[13] How is it possible that Rahman was emphasizing the distinction of "man from the rest of natural creation by the fact that God [states:] 'breathed My own spirit' into the first *'insan*" (15:29; 38:72; 32:9) and the female "fully-pledged personality," while limiting the meaning of *ma'* and *sulalah* to the male semen? Also, how could he be talking about "God fashion[ing] Adam out of a baked clay [of dark mud (*silsal*)] (15:26, 28, 33; 6:2; 7:12, etc.)" (Rahman 1980, 17) to differentiate Adam from the Jinn that was created of fire (15:27), while limiting such a process to the male progeny, knowing that God created everything in pairs (*azwaj*)?

A partial answer to the above questions could be found in other parts of Rahman's work (1980, 112), where *nafs* means the "inner person, i.e., the living reality of man [humankind]," but not separate from or exclusive of the body. Yet, Rahman's statement on creation—"when organized into a human being, produces an extract, *sulalah* (reproductive semen). When injected into the womb, this semen undergoes a creative process" (Rahman 1980, 17)—is still problematic. A partial answer could also be found in Wadud's (1999, 16) distinction between the creation of the first parents (Rahman's "Adam") and the creation of humankind (Rahman's "organized into a human being"). Yet, it is still not befitting to translate *sulalah* as reproductive semen or to interpret the *ma' mahin* as merely the male semen, ignoring both the female reproductive water and her active agency in the process. Unsatisfactory also is Wadud's explanation that Qur'anic "scarcity of details" about the meaning of "*zawj*" (a pair, a mate, or a dual) could have resulted in the traditional interpretation that male is the pri-mordial of human creation (1999, 17–20).

As I search for the reason why Rahman's explanation of human cre-ation was limited as such, or the reason why Wadud gave such a rationale for the ambiguous meaning of *zawj*, I am essentially attempting to further develop Rahman's thesis of rejecting the mechanical transmission of the message of the Qur'an, and Wadud's thesis of rejecting the male reading as the only legitimate one. But how could I do that pedagogically, with the new generation, when the very concept of the female existence is being compromised and, perhaps, divorced from its Qur'anic roots as being equally primordial to that of the male existence?

I am also trying to understand why Muslim women both past and present have stopped short of acquiring or becoming the "fully-pledged personality," but I do not see the answer coming clear and with confidence from either Rahman or Wadud, given their interpretation of the story of Creation. Nor do I find an answer in any work by those Muslim thinkers who purport to show the Qur'an as favoring gender justice. How could the new generation, then, be reading the Word of God?

Just as Fazlur Rahman stirred powerful feelings in his native Pakistan and elsewhere in the early 1960s by rejecting any notion that Muhammad was simply God's appointed vehicle through which the message was com-municated—in a mechanical manner—to humankind (Denny 1989, 98), I hope to awaken powerful feelings and thoughts to create more than just a new discourse among contemporary Muslims when I reject any explana-tion of the creation of humankind as being of the male order first.[14] My rejection is based on the Qur'anic concept of individual trust and account-ability, and—ironically—on Rahman's assertion that humankind could not receive the message of the Qur'an mechanically. Therefore, the pairs/mates of the human species have to be of the primordial nature in order for each to receive the Qur'an actively, since each will carry his or her own trust and accountability separately.

The Story of Creation, Morality, and *Taqwa*

We need to pose further questions to Rahman's and others' work concern-ing the story of Creation and its implications for morality and *taqwa:* how could the Qur'an speak of a physically secondary element in the human creation (the female element, ill-perceived as the womb that "passively" receives the semen, or as the broken rib of Adam), when the Qur'an in-

tends that each human individual be a primary element, an active participant in choosing the message, or a "fully-pledged personality"? Also, since
it is humankind as a whole (al-ʾinsan) who is given the trust, and who
chooses to carry or reject the message (Qurʾan, 4:1, 31; 33:72), how can the
pedagogical dynamics of such a message be carried by only one-half of the
pair, one-half of humanity?

As the Qurʾan does not accept the dualism of the physical and the spiritual, or the body and soul dichotomy, why was it possible for Rahman to
write about this Qurʾanic rejection of the body-soul dualism when addressing Muslim intellectual evolution from the perceptual to the
formulative (1980, 17), and yet in the same breath translate *sulalah* as the
male semen? Why did Rahman slip into this dichotomy of a male, then
female, order of creation, instead of translating *sulalah* as the "string of
processes"—"we made a clot out of the fertilized egg, and then we raised it
as another creature" (Qurʾan, 23:14)—or as "offspring" of both the male
and female elements, which is the more general meaning of the Arabic
word and is more in line with "We created you of a male and a female"?

If we accept such a dichotomy of a male order, then a female order, we
might be inferring that God could not create two sexes of the same clay,
even though we know that God created heaven and earth simultaneously.
Even if we explain this apparent dichotomy by using Wadud's (1999) differentiation between the creation of first parents and the creation of humankind as two subsequent processes, the fact that Wadud stops short of
investigating the meaning of *zawj*, mate/pair, might further cause us to
fall into the gendered interpretation.[15]

The structural change that I am proposing here, therefore, will be built
on making explicit the Qurʾanic view of a Muslim's religio-morality that is
conditioned on the ability of each individual to cognize it autonomously.
Although I am particularly concerned with the Muslim woman's morality,
I am using the Qurʾanic criterion of the moral, cognizant human being—
the conscientious human, the *muttaqi*—as the criterion. My method does
not rely on using gender as the unit of analysis—be it the biological identity of either sex or the social construct of gender, or as a "category of
thought" as used by Wadud. The *muttaqi* is the person who is able to
balance the "moral-religious exhortation" with reason to implement
Qurʾanic pedagogy as a process of learning, knowing, teaching, and living
Islam. Eventually, this pedagogical process will affect a change in the social
fabrics of the Muslim community, including the gender fabric.

I contend that *taqwa* was lost when Muslims disconnected the task of

Adam's (representing the cognizant humankind) learning the names of things (Qur'an, 2:31) from "coming to the Qur'an prepared to receive its commands, and—in the process—be inspired by its light." This disconnection has resulted from the assumption that "Adam" means the primordial male. Humankind's task, being a prerequisite to realizing the gift of the Qur'anic message, when made particular to the male, resulted in the assumption that Muhammad received the message mechanically and that Muslims only need to emulate the model of the Prophet and his male companions or the caliphs. Thus, my task is to dismantle these assumptions by reading the Qur'an pedagogically—a process not completed before, to my knowledge—as a moral message that requires reason and free will by each individual, and not only as a moral message that can be transmitted by example.

Note here that I am not ignoring the philosophical works on Islamic ethics, such as Ahmad Ibn Miskawayh's (320/932–421/1030) *Tahdhib al-Akhlaq* (1961), but I am concerned with the actual use of these ethics in the construction of knowledge and its pedagogical dynamics for each individual's religio-moral cognizance before moving on to policy making and to action, to practicing and living Islam. My pedagogical reading is intended to rejoin "Adam's learning the names of things" with the human realization of the gift of the Qur'anic message. It is my hope that the meaning of the woman's morality will be restored, from being under the guardianship of the male members of her household to being an autonomous religio-moral rational being, as the Qur'an intends, and, consequently, the active norm is not the hegemonic ethics of the social structure. Rather, *taqwa* would be the active norm as the Qur'an intended it to be.

By rejecting the above explanations (Rahman's and Wadud's) of the Creation story and their implications for morality and *taqwa*, I am also creating a new view of understanding Islam and the Muslim woman. By also rejecting the historically perceived notion that the morality of the Prophet's wives was a proxy morality limited to receiving mechanically what was communicated to them through the Prophet, I am asserting my earlier argument that there was no change in the perception of women's proxy morality among Muslims. If we accept such a notion of mechanical reception of the message, then my earlier argument will also be proven valid; that there was no change in the perception of the female as a "fully-pledged personality" and that no change has actually taken place in the social fabrics involving gender of the Medina community. Consequently, we may conclude that even the Qur'anic religio-moral mandates were not pedagogically perceived or practiced, then or now, because there was a separation "of the perceptive and formulative intelligence," as Rahman suggests. The demarcation between the conceptions of the "moral-religious exhortation" for males vis-à-vis females in later times compounded the effect of this separation.[16] I argue that the perceptive and formulative separation that Rahman talks about may have actually happened during the early Muslim community period, and not only after that period as Rahman suggests, because there was a demarcation between the conception of the moral-religious exhortation for males and for females. As a result, the pedagogical dynamics of knowledge construction was lost because this exhortation was separated from the individual moral-cognizance process. This separation and demarcation are evidenced in keeping the women, even the Prophet's wives, from participating in developing (theorizing) the sciences of *tafsir, Sunnah,* and *fiqh,* and consequently of policy making. The sporadic narratives that indicate 'A'isha was consulted on matters of *fiqh* and as a scholar (Afzalur Rahman 1987, 2:174–75), and the fact that she narrated "one fourth of the injunctions of the *shari'ah*," is not enough evidence to suggest her involvement in the construction of Islamic knowledge.

Lest I be misunderstood, I am basically questioning the proxy morality notion produced in history books (Muslim or non-Muslim) and affirmed in the narration about the Prophet's companions who happened to be related to him through marriage. The stories of Abu Bakr's asking 'A'isha, his daughter, to thank her husband, the Prophet, even when the Qur'anic revelation (24:11) was the base for vindicating her from being accused as unfaithful,[17] and that of 'Umar Ibn al-Khattab's nudging his daughter Hafsa for conspiring against her husband, the Prophet (Qur'an, 66:3) imply that these men (the most prominent companions of the Prophet) were exercising the proxy morality with their daughters, even when these daughters were the most trusted women of the time. The stories of 'Umar and 'Ali Bin Abi Talib's enjoining the Prophet to seclude his wives and his daughter Fatima, who was also the wife of Ali, provide other examples of the lack of change in perceiving woman's morality even as the Qur'an was revealed. This notion of proxy morality became considerably more emphasized after the prophetic period, and thus those stories were told in a manner to support it.[18]

In any case, we need to investigate how autonomous the Prophet's wives actually were. What was their moral stance (that is, their response to individual issues), and how binding is that stance for the rest of Muslim women then and now? Or should it be binding, since I have already clarified that the example is not to be made an ideal, and that it should remain an example only if not calling for mechanical emulation. Such an investigation requires a separate book, so I will limit the treatment of this matter to our present concern, the pedagogical significance of these three women: ʿAʾisha, Hafsa, and Fatima. The goal is to understand where Muslim interpretations of the role of these women have failed to reflect the Qurʾanic gender revolution. Thus, in the next chapter, I discuss the issue of proxy versus autonomous morality and its implications for the principle of modesty.

Autonomous Morality and the Principle of Modesty

Autonomous morality cancels the assumption of the proxy morality of women and can be achieved only when women consciously see the light of the Qur'an. Autonomous morality also does away with the assumption of segregated modesty and can only be achieved when women directly see the light of the world.

Muslims have often interpreted the two most controversial verses in the Qur'an (4:34 and 2:228) as earmarks for men's guardianship and superiority over women. Such an interpretation has not only resulted in a woman's loss of her self-identity with Islam, that is, she is perceived as having proxy religio-morality (complementarity), but also in the loss of identity of the generations that followed. Women have lost the ability to directly relate the message of the Qur'an, without intermediary interpretations, to the Qur'anic injunction for keeping its interpretation open in time and place, wherein each individual bears a responsibility and a right.

The claim of men's moral guardianship and superiority over women is based mainly on the concepts of *qawamah* and *darajah*, that is, responsibility toward the woman and a degree or an edge of an added responsibility in verses 4:34 and 2:228, respectively. In order to interpret them, we need to put these verses in the contexts of their chapters, as well as in the context of the Qur'anic concept of *khilafah*, and the meaning of God in such verses as "In the name of Allah, the Beneficent, the Merciful, and Guardian of the universe" (1:1–2). The *qawamah* in 4:34 only implies the domestic and financial obligation vis-à-vis the woman's biologically essential role of procreation. The variation in the *darajah* in 2:228 among men and women (God has bestowed differently among individuals) only indicates an added responsibility for the male when he initiates the divorce process. The relationship between the meanings of verses 4:34 and 2:228, and Islamic jus-

tice and human vicegerency, is summarized in verse 4:32, "Do not envi-
ously wish for that which God proffered on some and not on others. Men
and women, to each belong the works they have personally accomplished."
That is, although Islam regards men and women as created for different
but complementary biological functions, it does not specify these functions, nor does it generalize them to other intellectual, moral, or social
roles.

The practices of proxy morality and segregated modesty are equally
evidenced among today's young female scholars who may have surren-
dered their leadership initiative because of the commitment leading them
to do a task even when they do not agree with the leadership opinion.[1]
These practices often result in depicting woman's role as complementary
without actually thinking of the far-reaching implication of their (the
young female's) action or thought for the pedagogical dynamics of the
Qur'an. This complementarities mind-set, exemplified also in the reported
argument in *The Ideal Muslim Husband*,[2] cannot recognize the mandate
that each individual is entrusted with the Qur'an.

In the first section of this chapter, I also question the notion of early
Muslim women's proxy morality, including that of the Prophet's wives,
not only because of the historic manipulation of tradition exemplified in
the analysis of Nizam al-Mulk's *sira* of 'A'isha, the most beloved wife of
the Prophet (Spellberg 1988). Rather, I am questioning the practice of
proxy morality and rejecting the notion behind it for exactly the same
reason and precept that made Rahman reject the mechanical transmission
of the Qur'an to Prophet Muhammad. Rahman argues that the "'externality' interpretation [of the Qur'an], which became 'orthodox' is a product of
later interpretation, relying principally on *Hadith*" (Denny 1989, 99). Departing from Rahman's assumption that "orthodoxy" was the product of
later interpretations, I contend that it was the product of separating morality from cognition of (theorizing) the Qur'nic principles, and of differentiating between male and female morality, during the building of the first
Muslim community.

In the rest of this chapter I discuss the need to understand the Muslim
woman's religiosity/spirituality beyond the limited discussion of material
attire. That is, basic to changing perceptions about Islamic views of morality, modesty, and women's status is realizing the different meanings of
concepts related to public appearance and behavior for both women and
men. Exploring these concepts, beginning with the Qur'an and ending
with the political proponents and adversaries of special attire, is also an

educational process aimed at restoring justice to the Muslim woman. Although justice is equally expected from Muslims and non-Muslims, without a pedagogical and ethical understanding of these concepts, the debate and the intellectual molestation of Muslim women who choose or do not choose the customary attire will never produce attitudinal and conceptual change about Muslim women's morality. Regardless of the language with which the issue of the special attire has been told, and despite the thousands of interpretations and analyses that this subject has received, the intent of the present discussion is to bring the issue back to its Qur'anic pedagogical context. This intent, which, to my knowledge, has not previously been attempted, presents the related verses in the Qur'an within the context of its chapters and synthesizes the elements of contradiction and confusion that have surrounded the issue from the time of early interpretations (*tafasir* [pl. of *tafsir*]) to the present. This pedagogical reading also proposes new meanings and a different discourse for the relationship of attire to morality.

Proxy Morality and Autonomous Morality

The first proof of my argument—that "orthodoxy" was the product of separating morality from cognition, and of differentiating between male and female morality, during the building of the first Muslim community—is that gendered attitude was marginally changed. Perhaps there was a surface change in behavior, but because of separating morality from reason and because of differentiating between male and female morality, the perceptual and formulative processes were also separated. Consequently, by the next generation of Muslims, the pedagogical dynamics were totally lost in the face of the new social norms that were mostly introduced by the different converts to Islam. And, needless to say, the influx of large numbers of women slaves did enhance this sad state of affairs. Eventually, the pedagogical dynamics were completely lost to the legal codification in the attempts to preserve the "orthodoxy."

Rahman's fundamental assumption is that "the Qur'an at its core is a moral message, God's command" and that "in order to know what God requires of His creatures, human intellect must be applied" (Denny 1989, 99). If we accept both of Rahman's assumptions, that the Prophet did not receive the message mechanically and that it is necessary to apply human intellect to know the moral message, it would seem as if early Muslim women, including the Prophet's wives, were not included in the application of these Qur'anic fundamental assumptions, at least according to what is recorded in the history books. There is hardly a report in these books that any of these women exercised *qada* (jurisprudence reasoning) (Dutton 1999), which is a representation of exercising their intellectual gift in the process of executing their task.[3] 'A'isha herself is only referred to as the preserver or narrator of the Prophet's tradition, and is rarely mentioned as a jurist (*faqiha*) (Afzal-ur-Rahman 1982, 174–75).

Even when we do not take these history books at their face value, by surveying attitudes of contemporary Muslims (including women) about the female's morality, we can didactically conclude, first, that "the content of the message [of the Qur'an] was never to become the result of intimate internal psychological processes for these women," in line with Fazlur Rahman's assumption that that was the way for the Qur'an's moral message to be understood and applied, and, second, that Muslim societies have been harvesting the results of this lack of intimate psychological process. This harvest is evidenced in the entrenched attitudes toward women (and their perception of themselves), further excluding women, beginning with the knowledge-construction process and ending with the practice of leadership and inheritance. Fazlur Rahman himself asserts that this intimate process was necessary for Muslims to overcome the apprehension toward the "new" message of the Qur'an "at the perceptive level of moral-religious experience" and to move toward changing the social fabrics (Denny ibid.). Had these intimate processes taken place, we would have noticed some transformation in the attitudes concerning the Prophet's wives in their own right, and concerning gender in general—from the story of Creation to the recent rationales concerning Muslim woman's "modesty," segregation, and seclusion. Many Muslims exchange these rationales to the point that recently some newsgroups on the Internet have instated themselves as guardians over women's morality (discussed further in chapter 4). How else do we explain the practice concerning the female members of the Prophet's household, and concerning the rest of the Muslim women of his time, when even as some Qur'anic verses were revealed on behalf of these females, the patriarchal society at large was responding with resistance toward regarding them as partners in carrying the trust? Indeed, the society viewed women as secondary actors to men in carrying the task of the message (Afzal-ur-Rahman 1982, 173). Yes, there were some narratives of individual cases in which the Prophet affirmed his wives' and other women's intimate relation with the Qur'an, as well as their autonomous spiritual and intellectual participation in accepting the message (such as *bay'ah*, giving the oath, voting). Arabian women who chose the message of the Qur'an, and who accepted Muhammad as the Prophet of Islam, were given the opportunity to individually express their commitment (bay'ah) and to make the oath (that there is no god but God) before the Prophet. Women's oath was exercised separately (assigning a special day for the women to give the oath or to be taught about the foundations of Islam) in order to affirm the women's autonomy and primary role, not to segregate them. Regrettably, Muslims, in general, see this separation as a model for segregating men and women. Thus, without concerted efforts to integrate the results of this autonomous participation in the reconstruction of gender social fabrics, autonomy was left at the level of the religio-moral exhortation and was not conceptualized by Muslims to the point of changing attitudes.[4]

Muslims' general justifications for such shortcomings are that (i) the Prophet's behavior during *bay'ah* as such was a signal that the two sexes should remain segregated, or (ii) the social context then was not pertinent to such a "radical" change in the gender fabric, or (iii) the Qur'anic message was greater than just changing the gender social fabric. I reject these three justifications because, first of all, the Prophet's behavior is intended to give special attention to the women, emphasizing their autonomy as individuals who must carry the trust and the fact that they need to know and make a moral choice of accepting or rejecting the trust before they carry it. Also, women were participating in prayers and gatherings in the mosque together with men. Second, the Prophet's message was mainly "There is no god but God." Hence, how do we expect a woman to accept this total change in her worldview of the cosmos, all the while demanding that she make an exception for her male's household to remain as her moral guardian? Third, how is it possible for a message with such transformative principles to be applied without expecting resentment and change in the context, the social structure in which it is to be applied, and the attitude about woman, who represent half of the population?

Qur'anic Contexts and Meanings of *Libas, Saw'ah, Satr, Farj,
'Awrah, Zinah, Jilbab, Khimar, Ghita', Hijab,* and *Haya'*

To fulfill the purpose of human existence as the trustee according to the Qur'an, a Muslim woman would at least need to be acquainted with the Islamic system and its methodologies (*al-manhaj, al-nizam, al-shari'a,* the divine guidance and laws of nature) before she can turn the Islamic article of faith into action (Barazangi 1996, 91–92). This acquaintance is not to be limited to those who are literate, nor to those who read Arabic or those who acquire higher degrees in secular or religious institutions in the Western sense of literacy and higher education. To the contrary, understanding Qur'anic guidance and the Islamic worldview, relying mainly on the oral recitation of the Qur'an, is as simple as the ability to recite perceptually ("Read" or "*Iqra'*" [96:1] being the first revealed verse in the Qur'an), and to know the meaning of the article of faith (*La 'ilah 'illa Allah, Muhammad Rasool Allah*) stripped of the many layers of translations and meanings that might be class , ethnic , or gender-biased. This reading does not imply being cut off from previous knowledge and tradition, but rather keeping that knowledge and tradition in their proper place as secondary sources. Nor does this reading imply a denial of the centrality of Arabic to the believing Muslim's spiritual immersion in Islam, because Arabic is the only language of prayer, even when the praying individual does not understand the Arabic lexicon. Once the basic message of the text is communicated in the individual's own language, the language of the text becomes important as a tool of expression and as a means of uniting the individual with the source of the message, God.

The concepts and terms in the title of this section are often used individually and interchangeably in the context of discussing Muslim women's morality, modesty, and attire, but are never presented in a comprehensive relationship.[5] The most cited verses of the Qur'an when women's attire is discussed are in two sets. The first set is in chapter 24, titled "Al-Nur" (The Light). The second set is in chapter 33, titled "Al-Ahzab" (The Clans/The Confederate Tribes). In chapter 24, the Qur'an directs men to lower their gaze and guard their private areas (*furuj*, pl. of *farj*) in the context of commanding the believers not to slander women and to observe the women's privacy. The Qur'an also addresses women to do the same and, in addition, to throw their (customary) head covering (*khumur*, pl. of *khimar*) over their bosoms (*juyub*), and not to show their "ornaments" (*zinah*) except what might naturally appear and only to their husbands, fathers, fathers-in-law, sons, stepsons, brothers, nephews, or *their women* (24:31).[6]

The next set of cited verses is from chapter 33, wherein verse 53 emphasizes the privacy of the quarters (*buyut*) of Prophet Muhammad's wives: "and if you ask them [the wives] of any matter, then ask them from behind a curtain (*hijab*); that is cleaner (*'athar*) for your hearts and theirs" (33:53). Verse 59 discusses how to protect women's privacy, after prohibiting marriage to any of the Prophet's wives following his death, stating: "O Prophet, say to thy wives and daughters and the *believing women* that they draw their cloak (*jilbab*) close to them; so it is likelier they will be known [as such] and not molested" (I am emphasizing "believing women" as evidence that to talk to women from behind a curtain, as in verse 53, applies only to the Prophet's wives).

Although the rest of the concepts listed in the title above are present throughout these two chapters of the Qur'an and are relevant to the conditions of attire, privacy, and modesty, they are usually ignored. It would be a pedagogical mistake to continue to ignore these concepts and their relevance to attire. I will assume this task of incorporating them while rereading the guidelines of modesty and morality in the Qur'an in the hope of achieving a change in perception and attitude. I start with a historical overview, followed by the method of documentation, and then a pedagogical reading of Al-Nur and Al-Ahzab.

Historical Overview

The place in which these two chapters of the Qur'an were revealed was Medina; that is, after the migration of the Prophet and early Muslims from Mecca and during the formative period of the Muslim community (ca. 623). Early interpreters relied on chronological order of revelation as well as other documentation to assess the occasions of revelation and, consequently, to justify certain interpretations. I may reference some of the documentation for historical purposes, but I consider them only as secondary sources to the collective religio-moral rationality of the Qur'an.

Al-Nur and Al-Ahzab appear in many classical books of *tafsir,* such as *Marwiyat Ibn Hanbal fi al-Tafsir* (AD 780–855) (1994), *Tafsir al Nisa'i* (AD 830–915) (1990), *Al-Durr al-Manthur fi al-Tafsir al-Ma'thur* by al-Suyuti (AD 1445–1505), *Majma al-Bayan li 'Ulum al- Qur'an* of al-Tabarsi (d. AD 1153) (1958), and *Al-Gami': Tafsir al-Qur'an* of 'Abdu Allah Ibn Wahb (AD 743–812) (1993). Although these commentaries are often referenced more often than the Qur'anic text itself, I am only interested in why the men who have done these interpretations overlooked the pedagogical and ethical dynamics of the Qur'an, especially with reference to the issue of woman's attire. Of further notice is that only particular interpretations have recently became available in electronic text format, such as those of al-Qurtubi (790–852), al-Tabari (838–923), Ibn Kathir (1301–1373), and al-Jalalin (n.d.). I used these electronic sources mainly for the ease of searching for these concepts across interpretations.

The two Qur'anic chapters Al-Nur and Al-Ahzab have an equal number of appearances in the Hadith books as originally collected, such as *Sahih al-Bukhari, Muslim,* and so on. However, the appearance of the concepts related to attire (*hijab, jilbab, ghita'*) seems to multiply in the commentaries on these original collections. For instance, the concept *"ghita'"* appears only 22 times in *Sahih al-Bukhari* (AH 736–795), while it appears 102 times in *Fath al-B{a}ry fi Sharh Sahih al-Bukhari* (the commentary on al-Bukhari) (1996).

What concerns us here is the emphasis on the material meanings of *khimar* (head covering) and *libas/jilbab* (attire/cloak) that segregate the sexes, while ignoring the related metaphoric meanings such as *libas al-taqwa,* "the attire of taqwa" (Qur'an, 7:26) and *ghita' al-basar,* "the cover of consciousness or sight" (Qur'an, 50:22). Although these concepts appear in other chapters, only a few commentaries (such as the recent reading by Muhammad Shahrur, 1990), draw a relationship between them. Central to this relationship is the Qur'anic emphasis on human morality as the reason for the primordial woman's and man's awareness of their humanity and sexuality (as different from angels and animals) when they chose to eat from the "forbidden" tree. This act of choice made them also aware of each other's sexuality and, being moral beings, they came to feel the *haya'* (the need for privacy/cover) to maintain their individual autonomy. Thus, the metaphoric meanings of *libas al-taqwa* and *ghita' al-basar* are also intended to emphasize the vision and worldview of the believer that makes her or him understand these concepts as such, and differently from the nonbeliever, "You were unaware of this [meaning], and we have unveiled (*kashfna 'anka ghita'aka*) your unconsciousness, and now you are of a piercing sight" (Qur'an, 50:22). The multiplicity of narratives concerning the material interpretation of *"libas,"* away from the Qur'anic perspective, during certain historical eras and occasions, raises another concern when we assess the absence of pedagogical interpretation of the Qur'an and the absence of women from the Qur'anic interpretation, in general.

Method of Documentation

I searched Qur'anic injunctions within contextual occasions of the revelation (*asbab al-nuzul*) as narrated in the different books of *tafsir* and Hadith. Using the electronic text databases produced by Sakhr.com and its affiliates, I looked for related vocabulary in the rest of the two chapters and other verses, and compared interpretations as well as *asbab al-nuzul.* I used the Sinbad Browser (Arabic Netscape) to connect to the data bases of the Qur'an, to *Hadith Mawsu'ah* (The Encyclopedia of the Prophet's Tradition),[7] and to the four *tafasir:* al-Qurtubi, al-Tabari, Ibn Kathir, and al-Jalalin. The advantage of the electronic browser, besides providing the full text electronically, is the facilitation of sorting and matching for a systematic and comprehensive search. The primary results of this search show a multiplicity of interpretations and, hence, affirm my argument that these interpretations are not binding. This multiplicity also confirms my argument that it is possible and indeed necessary to reinterpret and attempt a new reading of the primary text, the Qur'an, in time and space. Finally, as most jurists relied on these *tafasir* when they made judgments—collected in the books of *fiqh* (jurisprudence) that became known collectively as *shari'a*, or Islamic law—one needs to understand why these interpreters and jurists missed the opportunity to "interpret the Qur'an into a really meaningful ethical and legal system," as Rahman suggests (2000, 62), and why in the process they also excluded women, missing the Qur'anic pedagogical dynamics that still affect interpretations of the Qur'an as a whole in the contemporary Muslim communities.

By following the Qur'an's reflective methodology—"Wouldn't they reflect [on the Qur'an], or are there locks on their hearts!" (Qur'an, 47:24); and "God has revealed the Book, coherent verses" (3:7); and "we should not take one another as gods" (3:64)—an average Muslim may be able to realize the totality of the Qur'anic message and its signs (indicators). For undertaking the responsibility of changing the view in reading the Qur'an from what has been practiced for centuries, as I am attempting here, one needs further steps, seeking both the rules of linguistic coherence (Shahrur 1990) of the text and the legal or moral aspect of interpretation, in addition to the endowed intelligence and intuitive recognition of the signs.

In doing the task of changing the view in Qur'anic reading, I am also guided by two levels of autonomy. The first, which is necessary for every Muslim, is the endowment of intelligence, ethics, and decision making needed to carry out the vicegerency consistent with God's absolute transcendence, but without accepting the misconception of human absolute, passive submission. The second level of autonomy—which is often confused when it is related to the woman's role—is the consideration of the socioeconomic order in Islam, wherein the family, instead of the tribe or the nation, is stipulated as the starting point to create a system of tranquility, independence, and partnership for the welfare of the principals (husband and wife) as well as the issue (the children). This combination of independence and partnership became highly confused when the interpretation of woman's attire and her role in this relationship, and in the society at large, was not understood in line with the principle that all creatures are equal and derive equality from a single pair created from a single soul (M. al Faruqi 2000).

The Qur'an states in 4:1: "O Humankind (*Ya'ayuha al-nas*), be conscientious of (*ittaqu*), or [in equilibrium with] your Guardian God (*Rabbakum*), who created you of a single [personal] entity (*nafs wahidah*). Created, of the same entity, its [grammatical feminine gender] mate (*zawjaha*), and from them scattered abroad many men and women, and be conscientious of God (*ittaqu Allah*) by whom you are accountable to one another, and the wombs (*al-Arham*); surely Allah ever watches over you." This verse reminds us of three major concepts; (i) *taqwa* as the criterion of the balanced relationship between the Creator and humanity, and between human independence and partnership; (ii) the creation from a single primordial entity of two independently ethical and legal persons, woman and man; and (iii) the reverence of the wombs as the basis for determining human interaction and relationship on all levels, raising this reverence almost to the level of reverencing Allah as the source of knowledge and value. We will see later why the guarding of the wombs is basic, to the point of being reverenced. Could it be due to the fact that they are made the center for just human socioeconomic relations and an anticapital accumulation system of inheritance?

By following the pedagogical meanings of *taqwa*, I am asserting that the Qur'an is not only the primary source of Islamic principles but also of guidance (*huda*), not merely a source of law in the sense of rigid rules and regulations. Although the moral binding of the Qur'an may become legal in the sense that a person feels obliged to follow its guidance once she or he accepts the Islamic worldview of "There is no god but God," imparting this guidance into action varies in space and time, as the prophet Muhammad's varied (as told by different narrators on different occasions and in different places) extrapolations of Qur'anic injunctions indicate. Furthermore, by imparting the guidance into a pedagogically dynamic system that will move the intuitive human reasoning of right and wrong into a universally applicable ethical system, I am asserting the essentiality of seeing the two moral and legal entities, the woman and the man, as two intellectually and spiritually independent entities before they can become partners in the family relationship.

Thus, to see the socioreligious relations of the individual female only in a lens complementary to the males in her household is misleading, and has led to injustices to the female entity because she was always seen as secondary, instead of being primary in the family relations. Such injustices are reflected particularly in the perceptions and practice of the attire and the segregated modesty, as well as in policy making and inheritance practices.

Pedagogical Reading of Al-Nur and Al-Ahzab

Once we apply the overarching principle of the Qur'an as *huda,* its guidelines about modesty and morality and their relationship to women's attire become simple and clear. Contrary to the emphasis by the *tafasir* on the idea of covering women's bodies to avoid tempting men, the meanings of material and metaphoric concepts of *libas, satr, jilbab, hijab, ghita',* and *khimar* are transformed. These concepts become instruments intended to change the view of human relations, primary among them the relation to women. The changed view is intended to move the Islamic community from basing its relationships on tribal loyalty as dominated mainly by a male lineage, and instead to introduce the female as a principal in the familial socioeconomic and religious relations. This view starts with the story of Creation and touches on all aspects of life.

First, the Qur'anic view emphasizes the concept of *satr* (to hide or to cover) human *saw'ah* (s. of *saw'at,* the areas of the body that biologically mark maleness and femaleness), to remind humankind of morality as the character that distinguishes humans from other creatures. This morality is guarded by human *haya'* (quest for privacy for self-dignity and respect for the other partner even when approaching the feeling of lust), in contrast to animals whose relations are determined only by their biological needs and the natural laws.

Second, the Qur'anic view emphasizes the concept of *hifdh al-farj* to mark the criterion for human biological relations. The emphasis on reverencing the wombs (4:1) and on covering the bosoms (24:31), for example, is intended mainly to change the status of the woman from mere carrier of the child—who could be adopted or rejected by the tribe—to an active partner in the reproduction process, as well as a principal in determining blood and marriage relations. The Qur'an reads: "Say to the believing men to lower their gaze and guard their *furuj,* the area of private parts, that is purer (*azka*) for them, and Allah knows what they do" (24:30). Yet, when the guidelines were directed to women, they were elaborated to present the effect of the woman's womb (the source of blood and marriage relations) and bosoms (the source of lactation relations) on determining the socioeconomic legitimacy of all the male relatives: "and say to the believing women to lower their gaze and guard their *furuj,* and not display their *zinah* except what appears thereof, and to draw their *khumur* over their bosoms, and not display their *zinah* except to their husbands, fathers or fathers-in-law, their sons or stepsons, their brothers or nephews, their women or slaves, their male attendants who lack [sexual] vigor or children who have not yet developed lust or awareness of women's private parts (*'awrat al-nisa'*), and they should not stamp with their feet so their *zinah* become apparent, and ask for forgiveness from Allah, all of you, oh believers [males and females] that you may win Allah's grace" (24:31).

I will focus my pedagogical reading of these verses and related verses on two major issues. I begin by presenting the different meanings of *'awrah* (s. of *'awrat*), *zinah,* and *farj* that are often discussed as if they referenced the same thing. Next, I will discuss the meanings of *hijab, jilbab,* and associated concepts, such as *libas, khimar,* and *ghita'.*

What becomes obvious in the above verses and related verses in the same chapter, chapter 24, and in chapter 33 is the following:

First, the concept of *zinah* is prominent, meaning "beauty" or the area of the body that is customarily beautified by "ornaments," such as the neck, the ears, the arms, and the ankles. These areas could inadvertently be exposed during daily functions and, therefore, designate one level of privacy and protection. Then there is the second level of *zinah*—the bosoms and related "functions or family relations" that may appear only before seven categories of men and the collective category of "their *nisa'.*" These categories are in line with the Islamic perspective of modesty being a preventive measure for guarding the woman's privacy so as to protect the wombs, and blood and lactation lineage for securing a just inheritance system, not merely to protect against sexual temptation.[8] One only needs to read the first twenty-five verses of chapter 24 to understand the context: to stop those who would slander widows and orphans so as to deprive them of their inheritance and fair play. These twenty-five verses are followed by four verses (26–29) specifying what kind of men are suited for a kind of women, urging the believers not to enter others' homes without permission. These verses contextualize the specification as to what is permissible to look at once entering others' homes, including the gaze toward the other sex.

Second, the concept of guarding private areas (*hifdh al-farj*) is emphasized for both males and females, and since it is not at the same level of *zinah* for the females, the latter is explicitly added: "and say to the believing women to lower their gaze and guard their private area and not display their *zinah* except what appears thereof." The Qur'an does not repeat *zinah* three times in different linguistic and contextual discourses in vain. Therefore, the concept of not displaying the areas of the *zinah* are intended to emphasize the different parts of the body, and different levels of "ornamentation" (clothing) for different places and times of the day. In addition, *'awrah* (parts of the body that should be covered by both men and women even in the presence of close relatives) is also intended for different levels of modest behavior for all family and domestic dwellers, including children. This concept is addressed again in verses 24:58–59, wherein believers are told to educate children (those who have or have not reached puberty), slaves, and servants to ask for permission before entering the private quarters during three times of the day (before dawn, during the siesta, and after evening prayer). The Qur'an calls these times *'awrat*, meaning that they are to be observed as private times for the mature women and men. Also, *'awrah* is forbidden from being exposed except to the spouse. The Qur'an clearly distinguishes between *farj*, *'awrah*, and *zinah* as three places in the human body that call for different levels of covering with different guidelines to observe their privacy or sanctity. Thus, the level of covering, or privacy, or protection, differs with these three different concepts, and according to age, sex, and blood, lactation or marriage relations, as well as the age and sex of those in domestic attendance, and according to the time of the day and the different quarters of one's home. It is very critical to ask the following question now: If indeed the Qur'an intended to declare the entire woman as " *'awrah*," that is, she is forbidden to appear before people who do not belong to any of the eight categories mentioned in Al-Nur, 24:31, as the general perception and practice suggest, then what is the meaning of *zinah*, and why are there different levels of *zinah*, and different categories of men, places, and times for covering the *zinah*?

Third, the different meanings and levels of protection in these concepts are further evidenced in the verse "Women past the age of child-bearing and those who are not hopeful of marriage because of disability may lay aside their clothes but without exposing their *zinah*, and they ought to purify themselves, that is better for them, and Allah is the Hearer, the Knower" (24:60).

Central to interpreting Islamic guidance in general, and this verse in particular, are the meanings of the rationale of justification (*'illah*), and the preventive measure (*radd al-dhari'ah*). Both of these principles are necessary to make practicable the Qur'anic principles of morality, modesty, and justice. As explained by Maysam al Faruqi (2000), the nature of Islamic law is such that one cannot treat it either as a simple system of precedence, or as a set of rules the letter of which must be respected. If we read verse 24:60 with the above notions, principles, and understanding of the nature of Islamic law in mind, it becomes clear that clothes were intended as a measure of protection for the purpose (*'illah*) of assurance in determining the family lineage to guarantee justice in inheritance. Thus, the outer garments (*jalabib*) in 30:33, or the head covers (*khumur*) in 24:31, are all intended to guard the wombs and the bosoms as the places that determine lineage, more so than to cover the body of the woman ipso facto. The prophetic tradition that allows a woman to remove her *khimar* before a prospective husband is further evidence for my explanation. Modesty is intended to protect the family lineage, and since the two principals in family life are the woman and the man, their acceptance of each other is of a higher value than absolute observation of attire restrictions merely for the sake of covering the woman's body.

Perplexing Meanings and Practices of Al-Nur and Al-Ahzab

It is perplexing how the three principles of morality, modesty, and justice in family relations have been reversed in actual practice among Muslims. We see, for instance, the practice of arranged marriage in which the two partners do not see each other before the consummation of marriage. We also see women become more conservative in their attire at older age, thinking that it is more pious to do so as they get older. Finally, we see more emphasis on the woman's overall covering than on her male relatives' observing the guidelines of lowering their gaze and respecting *'awrat* times and places when they stay in these women's homes beyond the normal visitation times, contrary to the Qur'anic instructions.

Therefore, a woman who self-identifies with the Qur'anic worldview realizes that Islamic teachings regarding modesty are neither rigid nor intended to make her feel guilty of tempting the males, and neither is following these guidelines a function of control, submission, segregation, or restriction of action, as usually perceived and practiced. These guidelines are for individual chastity and social protocol (*hishmah*), with the aim of respecting privacy and lineage. If these teachings are not internalized as such, they can also not be fully realized in practice, even if the individual's behavior suggests otherwise. A woman who practices wearing a cloak and a head covering without understanding the above modesty principle, for instance, is not practicing Islam, but a social custom. On the contrary, a woman who internalizes Islamic principles of morality and justice demands the observation of the modesty principle not in terms of its prohibitive, rigid law for the females, as is rationalized by some male interpreters, but in terms of the guiding principles of the Qur'an on morality and modesty for both males and females. She would also realize that the claim that the male's 'awrah is only that area between his waist and knees is, therefore, misleading because it is taken out of the context of chastity. Since the general norm of the time was that male lineage was the only principle in tribal inheritance, the meaning of *hifdh al-farj* took on the limited meaning of sexuality and the specific areas of sexual desires. In addition, since the man's breast has no lactation function, men were not required to cover their bosoms as women were. Covering women's bosoms was to protect the familial lactation relations that affect the rules of inheritance as well as marriage. Finally, as the *khimar* is a customary practice for both males and females in the desert environment and prior to Islam,[9] to impose its use only for the female's head, and to extend the meaning of *khimar* to *hijab* (a curtain, a divider) to separate males from females, results in injustice both for the female and for the Qur'an, because it means stripping women of their primary status in the family's socioeconomic structure as well as misreading back into the Qur'an something that the Qur'an does not contain.

The goal of Islamic education, and of this book, is *taqwa*, that is, balancing individual and social norms (*'urf*) with natural laws and within the Qur'anic guidelines. Thus, one aim of the book is to enable the individual to draw the line between the mere following of precedence (*taqlid*), on the one hand, and of social customs and understanding of the *'urf* in time and place, and understanding the Islamic principles and their rationale, on the other. Autonomous morality with deeper knowledge prevents the woman from feeling guilty (which is not a constructive, nor an intended, goal in Islamic ethics) about not following a social custom, if she determines that the particular custom may cause injustice. The Qur'an teaches us not to inflict on ourselves what God has not: "*Latukallaf nafs 'illa wusa'ha*" (A soul may not be required what a soul cannot bear) (2:233, 286; and a similar version in 6:125; 7:42; 23:62; 65:7). Such inflection may render a certain guideline irrelevant in a particular space and time, particularly when, for example, justice is threatened.

The same is true for understanding the relationship of autonomous morality and modesty. Why is it that the notion of woman's attire is not understood and practiced in the same manner of understanding as other injunctions of the Qur'an? Isn't the idea of modesty intended to avoid mixing the lineage? Surely, this can still be secured without causing cultural and factional wars because of different interpretations or observations of woman's attire and morality. Equally important is that we restore justice to the woman by restoring respect to her as a principal partner in determining the level of modesty necessary for the circumstances, and by retaining her autonomy in understanding and practicing Islam.

It is further perplexing how Muslims accepted suspending the practice of fasting during travel, illness, or pregnancy and child delivery and nursing, without understanding the practice of attire within the same principles of justice and autonomy, and the overarching perception of the Qur'an as *huda*, guidance. Furthermore, Muslims ignore the fact that external measures, such as clothing, do not give others the authority to judge a woman's character, or to impose customary restrictions on her, while allowing men to violate the same Islamic guidance. The criterion of *taqwa* reminds us that clothing is only one symbol of accepting the principle of modesty. Thus, the suspension of this external symbol in the proper *'urf* of the time and place does not necessarily mean that the person is guilty or a "sinner." The balanced Islamic identity is that which recognizes when and how to act on an Islamic guidance.

4

Gender Equality (*al-Musawah*) and Equilibrium (*Taqwa*)

Taqwa, or the balance of individual conscientious moral choice and social action, was lost in the process of "religious education." Early Muslims became aware of their self-identity with the worldview of Islam through the religio-moral exhortation of the Meccan injunctions, shifting their view as a result of the dynamics of the Qur'anic revelation. With some exceptions, as this first generation of Muslims began experiencing the formulative reasoning of the Islamic worldview through the Medina revelation, they were applying Islamic injunctions without going through the process of generating meaning or developing policy theories. Consequently, in the absence of the direct experience of the religio-moral exhortation, and given their departure from the communities of Medina and Mecca, the following generations of Muslims may have missed this vigor of the Qur'anic dynamics. Similarly, perhaps by being born to Muslim parents, they may have come to Islam automatically; the majority of Muslim youths of today did not go through this intense religio-moral exhortation, either. Yet, as the vigor of the theological and intellectual work of a number of contemporary women has begun to generate new meanings, we have started to observe changes in the social fabrics, such as in the American Muslim communities and in the American religious landscape in general. This practical change may lead these women to perceptual change in approaching the religio-morality, in contrast to what has happened to previous generations of Muslims. The course that this change may take will depend, nevertheless, on the view by which the Qur'an is interpreted. My proposed pedagogical reading of the Qur'an is a response to this undercurrent taking place at the grassroots level. Hence, my task is to facilitate this practical undercurrent within the self-identity framework in order to ensure a shift toward self-realization instead of self-sacrifice.

Nasr (1995, 463) argues that "the sacred law (*shariʿa*) in Islam involves not only principles but also their application to daily life in the form of legal codifications." I must disagree with Nasr's argument, because it is this legal codification that stripped Islam of its Qurʾanic conscientious morality and pedagogical dynamics. The sacredness of Islamic *Shariʿa* as intended in the Qurʾan is limited to the Qurʾan, and does not extend to what is known as Islamic law.[1] Only the explication of the Qurʾan in the prophetic authentic tradition was what Rahman (1966) calls the "moral-religious exhortation step." Yet, once *shariʿa* is extended to include the different juristic and contemporary interpretations as part of the sacred, Nasr's argument no longer applies. It does not apply because, as Rahman asserts, as Muslims moved into the formulative-intelligence step, they disconnected the formulative from the perceptive intelligence. This organic connection was severed, in my opinion, when one-half of the human pair, the female, was made a religious burden, socially and morally dependent, and almost intellectually and intuitively nil. As Renard (1994, 32) suggests, the Qurʾanic principles explain not only the need for and the priority of Islamic higher learning, for example, but also the unity of Islamic philosophy despite theological and historical diversity.

In order to explain the Qurʾanic pedagogical dynamics in action—including the elements needed for self-realization—I view *Islamic education* as a process of religio-moral and cognitive development, while *religious education* is the process of formulizing Islam into dogma. Islamic education follows the process of research-theory-policy (balancing individual conscientious moral choice and social action, or *taqwa*), while religious education follows the process of research policy (not allowing the individual to participate in acquiring awareness of, and making meaning of the relationship between responsible reasoning and social action).

In the words of Jim Cummins (1999), in the research-theory-policy process, the validity of a theory tests its predictive model against the patterns observed in the phenomenon—perceptual and social change in this case. While the first generation of Muslim jurists may have followed this process, they lost the community's perceptual input (theorizing) when they limited their own activities to legal enactment. That is, the jurists may have tested the validity of the predictive model against the assumed needs of the communities, but they were not testing their model against actual interests and attitudes of these communities.[2] Meanwhile, later generations of Muslims who merely followed this legal enactment—the formulative jurisprudence process—reduced the process back to research policy, neither testing the jurists' theories against the phenomenon in time and place, nor allowing any theorizing for fear of contaminating the original text; this was negatively compounded by the fact that they limited the jurisprudence process to the male members of the elite.

I have already redefined Islamic religio-morality pedagogically and its meaning for the Muslim woman's morality and education in modesty (chapter 3). To further clarify my views and to support my earlier arguments, in the remainder of this chapter I present the work of some contemporary Muslim female scholars and their disciples. The lack of leadership initiative in affirming woman's autonomous religio-morality among these scholars seems to contribute to the separation between the formulative and the perceptive in some of their work, even when they are writing about the favorable Qur'anic status for women.

The Argument for Equity versus Equality

Despite the significant contribution of her literary reading of the Qur'an, 'A'isha 'Abd al-Rahman makes several contradictory assertions when attempting to explain the difference between equality and equity. Regrettably, these assertions are reiterated in different forms and different levels, knowingly or unknowingly, by both Amina Wadud (1999) and Azizah al-Hibri (1982 and 1997).

'Abd al-Rahman, after an eloquent argument for the need to revive the Islamic woman's rights, states that liberation "for the new [Muslim] woman is not equality (al-musawah), because such a woman cannot be confusing the natural biological differences between males and females, nor the social differences between a man and a woman [with the concept of absolute equality]. Equality for this new woman does not go beyond the equitable rights and obligations (al-huquq wa al-wajibat al-muta-kafi'a)."[3] This assertion further complicates the matter when 'Abd al-Rahman (1967, 12) goes on to say: "The concept of equality (or lack thereof) in the book of Islam is about the good and the bad . . . and of knowledge and ignorance, not about maleness and femaleness." How could I, conscious of the Qur'anic meaning of equality, explain 'Abd al-Rahman's contradictory meanings to the new generation? It is indeed true that gender is neither central to the issues of equality and taqwa, nor as prominent as self-identity is with the Qur'an and Islam. Yet, the limited biological differences in the procreation role do not make all natural dispositions different, nor do they dictate social differences.

What is it that makes a scholar of 'Abd al-Rahman's stature and skills, bringing about a completely new reading of the Qur'an, stop short of realizing that one of the important aspects of the Qur'anic social revolution is the equality and justice between males and females?[4] As Fazlur Rahman asserts: "Equality of the sexes is instituted in the Qur'an (4:1, 7; 60:12; 49:10; 96:1–4) for a Muslim society to achieve *'Adl* [justice] and *Qist* [fair play]" (1996, 17).

A similar example to 'A'isha 'Abd al-Rahman's lack of realization of equality as one aspect of Qur'anic social justice is found in Amina Wadud's (1999, 9) argument that "with regard to some practices, the Qur'an seems to have remained neutral: social patriarchy, material patriarchy, economic hierarchy, the division of labor between males and females within a particular family." How could we attribute *neutrality* to the Qur'an, something that was subsequently read into the Qur'an by a number of interpreters, when we know that the Qur'anic revolution was in essence a revolution against all biases—gender, class, race, and so on?

It seems that this lack of realization—which in a sense is also a lack of leadership initiative in changing the existing misconceptions and the contextual social structure, the social fabrics of the time—has resulted from the two scholarly attempts (by 'Abd al-Rahman and Wadud) to emphasize the universality of the Qur'anic religio-moral principles vis-à-vis the culture-specific practices. While wishing to maintain the neutrality (with regard to gender, class, race) of the principles and in the text of the Qur'an, these two scholars and others who share a similar understanding may have overlooked the fact that these principles were intended to change the practice and its underlying assumptions *exactly because* the practices were keeping the considerations for cultural-specific prescriptions (of how to function according to one's sex) at the same level of Qur'anic guidance. The following two paragraphs quoted from Wadud (1999, 8) clarify my point. She states: "The Qur'an acknowledges that men and women function as individuals and in society. However, there is no detailed prescription set on how to function, culturally." She nevertheless adds, "Gender distinctions and distinct gender functions contribute to the perceptions of morally appropriate behaviour in a given society. Since the Qur'an is moral guidance, it must relate to the perceptions of morality—no matter how gender-specified—which are held by individuals in various societies" (9). It is exactly this last phrase of Wadud that is problematic, as, unfortunately, she falls short of elaborating and explaining her intended meaning. While it is true that prior perception of morality will affect the human's understanding of the Qur'an as a moral guidance, it is also this prior perception that the Qur'an intended to change. How else could a woman change her worldview from regarding herself as secondary to the males in her household to that of viewing herself as being guarded only by the guidance of the Qur'an? In reality, most Muslims did not change their prior perception of morality, especially regarding the morality of women (from that of the woman being guarded by her male household to the one of woman being autonomous); thus my argument that the Qur'anic gender social revolution hardly, if ever, took place.

'A'isha 'Abd al-Rahman and Amina Wadud could have asserted the neutrality and universality of the Qur'an with respect to the content of the religio-moral principles. That is, they could have done so by explaining the "no Particularism" in Qur'anic principles and the standard of *taqwa* in interpreting morality principles, as the case was made, for example, in my earlier work (Barazangi 1996, 80–81). In addition, and in accordance with the above principles, they could have also asserted the Qur'anic emphasis on changing the existing social fabrics (the contexts in which the principles are to be applied, similar to what took place in the Medina community with the onset of Islam) in order to achieve gender justice. This social justice is achievable only when women take on the same status of religio-moral cognizance that is given to men, regardless of the social context. It is this process of making a learner aware and able to understand (to theorize) the Qur'anic *apropos* principles (the declarative knowledge) from its rules for interpretations and the conditions for application (the procedural knowledge and its context) that constitutes "a pedagogical reading of the Qur'an" (see chapter 5).

When a Muslim learner is able to see the relationship between the two types of knowledge—that is, the religio-moral exhortation of the Qur'an represented in the principles, on the one hand, and her own cognizance of the meanings of these principles stripped of prior interpretations, on the other—and when she changes both her prior conceptions and her practices accordingly, then we can claim that self-learning of Islam and self-identification with the Qur'an have taken place. This is what I call "Islamic education" as opposed to religious education. The next step, the self-realization, takes place when the learner changes the structure of the context in which she is applying or practicing these principles without going outside the Islamic worldview. Then and only then can she become a person who has participated in the knowledge-construction of the society. Without these steps she may not achieve self-identity with, nor will she be able to be the interpreter of the Word of God (nor any text for that matter) to the next generation, and neither will she change history or develop her capacity for *autonomous intentionality*. Intention or conscientious moral choice is a pivotal concept in the Qur'an and a prerequisite to any action before it can be labeled "Islamic."

Relating *al-Musawah* to *Taqwa*

A further complication arises from 'A'isha 'Abd al-Rahman's assertions as she goes on to say: "By going back to the core of Islam, we will free our conception of equality (*al-musawah*) from these contemporary confusions [of women's liberation]. Thus the woman who has a sound natural endowment (*fitra*) would acknowledge that man has the natural and the legal (*shar'i*) right to have a *qawamah* over her." 'Abd al-Rahman makes the same unfortunate mistake as other interpreters by wrongly quoting the verse about *darajah* (degree) to affirm *qawamah* (superiority or guardianship), whereas these two verses (2:228 and 4:34) represent two different contexts (see chapter 3).[5] Furthermore, she quotes exclusively the last part of verse 2:228, which speaks of men having a degree over women, taking it out of the context of the verse. The context of this verse limits the meaning to that of a man having a [extra] degree of responsibility when he initiates the divorce process (Barazangi 1997, 53). Instead, 'Abd al-Rahman (1967, 12) elaborates on the traditional interpretation of the concept of *qawamah*, adding: "It is about time that men understood that *qawamah* in the Qur'an is not merely related to maleness, like in the verse of inheritance. Rather it is, in the Islamic conception, a right to manhood, and there is nothing we like more, we the free Muslim women, than acknowledging to our men this *qawamah* with ease and comfort."

What is problematic in the above statements is that 'Abd al-Rahman confuses what is Qur'anic with what is "Islamic" (that is, what has been canonized as Islamic). The other problem is that she confuses the difference in the biological male responsibility toward the female in the procreation process (the economic support vis-à-vis bearing and nursing the child), with the difference in the social upholding of manhood above womanhood. When she refuses to use maleness as the criterion, while she accepts this criterion for interpreting the verse of inheritance, she is actually overlooking the fact that what has been driving the misinterpretation of the concept of *qawamah* is exactly the excuse for the male to get the extra share of the inheritance (Arkoun 1994). That is, interpreting *qawamah* as male guardianship over the female was justified by male economic responsibility, despite the fact that this responsibility is bound by the particular familial relation and not by the fact of maleness or femaleness. This traditional interpretation of *qawamah* also justifies the interpretation that a male has twice the female share of inheritance because a man spends from his extra share of inheritance as the guardian of a woman. Such interpretations are upheld by Muslim male elites to justify both the standard interpretation of the extra share for the male—which is actually not across the board for all males, but only in the case of brother and sister, or husband and wife (Qur'an, 4:11–13)—and the guardianship for the male.[6] Unfortunately, both Azizah al-Hibri and Amina Wadud repeat—knowingly or unknowingly—'A'isha 'Abd al-Rahman's explanation to a certain extent. Since I have discussed some of Wadud's meanings earlier, I will only refer the reader to her treatment of the concepts of *darajah* and *qawamah* (1999, 66–74), while focusing on al-Hibri's related work.

Although al-Hibri refuses the standard interpretation of financial maintenance, changing the meaning of *qawamah* from "maintenance" to "moral guidance," she—perhaps unknowingly and unintentionally—reinforces both the traditional conception of male guardianship and of woman's proxy morality, while at the same time depriving women of their God-given right to financial support by their male household. She states that "since men are '*qawwamun*' over women in matters where God gave some of the men more than some of the women, and in what the men spend of their money, then clearly men *as a class* are not '*qawwamun*' over women *as a class*" (1982, 218, her emphasis). As she proceeds to list the two conditions for *qawamah* in the following paragraph, she again associates the financial obligations of men toward women with their moral guardianship over the women, stating that "if both [conditions] obtain, then all that entitles him to caring for her and providing her with moral guidance."

In the process of arguing the difference between specific cases of some men and some women to prove that "clearly men as a class are not '*qawwamun*' over women as a class," she seems to overlook the following.

First, *qawamah* means to stand up to a responsibility, not to stand out in rank. The responsibility of males is clearly financial, and it is only such, without entitling them to anything except partnership in marriage, parenting, and kinship. Hence, all men are financially responsible toward the women in their household, regardless of the two conditions that al-Hibri lists: "that the man be someone whom God gave more in the matter at hand than the woman, and that he be her provider." Independent from the question whether the stature and the wealth of the man are superior to those of the woman, or vice versa, the man is responsible for providing the woman's livelihood if she is a member of his household (as mother, daughter, wife, grandmother, and so on).

Second, the Qur'anic verse 4:32, "Do not envy each other, for men a share of what they have earned and for women a share of what they have earned," explains the prior verses indicating different inheritance shares for different categories of family members. It acts as a reminder that the extra share of inheritance for some categories (for a husband more than for a wife, and for a brother more than for a sister) are earned by these categories of men because they are financially responsible (they are expected to stand up to their responsibility) toward these categories of women.

Al-Hibri also quotes the verse "the believers, men and women are *awliya'* (guides) one of another" (Qur'an, 9:71), without alluding to the fact that "*wilaya*" (n.) is preconditioned by woman's moral autonomy. Even as she quotes the same verse in order to refute the standard interpretations and to assert the woman's "right to self-determination," she overlooks this precondition, failing to introduce a new criterion for changing the biased laws, and the conception of women's morality from that of a proxy morality to the autonomous morality. Instead, she directs her attention to some traditional rules of interpretation (to the procedural knowledge, rather than to the declarative knowledge, the principles), agreeing with one of the '*ulama*'s accepted fundamental criteria for changing laws" —laws change as times and places change" (al-Hibri 1982, 219), without recognizing that these changes do not mean much as long as the basic premises in interpreting *qawamah*, that is, seeing women's morality as proxy morality, have not changed.

Why is it that al-Hibri translates or interprets the same Arabic word "*ba'd/ba'dahun*" to mean "some of" in the first verse (4:34), while she generalizes it to mean "all of the believers" in the other verse (9:71)? Is this only a matter of the different preposition attached to each of them, or the grammatical structure (as she argues in the first case), or is it because she is being demure about taking the leadership initiative in refusing the whole concept of men's guardianship over women as traditionally interpreted? I need not dwell much on this matter because I do not wish to diminish the significance of the contribution of these respected scholars. Yet it strikes me that they are either avoiding controversy, or have not actually used their capacity for autonomous intentionality in their identification with the Qur'an and with Islam in the sense that I described earlier.[7] Nevertheless, in fairness to the subject, and to clarify my thesis, I must point to the manner in which the contradiction about woman's morality takes place in other writings of al-Hibri.

In her elaborate work on Islam, law, and custom (1997, 32), al-Hibri reexamines the concept of *qawamah*. After a painstaking explanation of the Arabic linguistic and language structure of the phrase on *qawamah*, using evidence from traditional interpretations, she concludes with the following: "The complex phrase was revealed in an authoritarian/patriarchal society that the Prophet was attempting to civilize and democratize. Consequently, it should be viewed for what it really is. It is a *limitation* on men which prevents them from assuming automatically (as many did then) oppressive authoritarian roles with respect to women" (her emphasis). She goes on to explain that this phrase tells them they may guide and advise only those women they support financially and then only when certain conditions are obtained. In addition to the fact that al-Hibri contradicts her earlier (1982) explanation that the guardianship is moral and not financial, there is another major problem in her 1997 explanation.

What is problematic in such an explanation is that it misses the whole meaning of the Qur'anic gender revolution—that the entire view of male-female structure be changed so that no limitation or advance privilege is ascribed to any group under any circumstances, and that individual morality stands on its own a priori. Without this morality being recognized as such and practiced pedagogically, the practice of mutual consultation and protection of one another's morality (*wilaya*, which al-Hibri emphasizes from verse 9:71) may neither be understood nor fully applied. I should also once again bring attention to the point I raised earlier regarding Wadud's "neutrality" of the Qur'an. As the Qur'anic principles are universal for all times and places, we cannot view the phrase "for what it really is," as al-Hibri suggests, to be only situational to the context of the society then, which Wadud also seems to suggest. Thus, the verse is not only limiting the patriarchal authoritarianism of certain individuals, or in one context only, but is actually abolishing this authoritarianism *apropos*.

Other evidence for my argument is found in the contradictory example al-Hibri uses to show that her analysis was "consistent with the Hanafi and Maliki views in that a woman may include in her marriage contract conditions that would give her greater rights and freedom within the marriage, including the right to divorce" (1997, 32–33). How can al-Hibri accept such an interpretation when it is based on the perception that a woman is not free to execute her endowed rights to marriage and divorce unless she writes them in her marriage contract? Perhaps al-Hibri was trying to show that there was a precedent in Muslim jurisprudence that allows women to write certain conditions into their marriage contracts. But by doing so, she unconditionally surrenders to this traditional inter-pretation that overlooks the basic principle of women's inherited rights to exercise marriage and divorce with autonomous intentionality.

It is even more problematic for the pedagogy of the Qur'an when al-Hibri narrates, in support of her argument, the controversy that took place against Toujan al-Faysal, a TV journalist who was elected as a member of the Jordanian Parliament in the mid 1990s (Brand 1998, 105). In her at-tempt to assert her rights, al-Faysal had included the condition for the right to divorce in her marriage contract. This practice is thought by con-temporary Muslim feminist lawyers to eliminate or modify the general misinterpretation and jurisprudence that a woman may ask for divorce only through the court, and only if she gives back her legal and moral right to the dowry that was given by the spouse at the time of signing the mar-riage contract. It has been proven that this recent practice by some women at the legal level only, without an actual change in the meaning of *qawamah* from what has been interpreted and practiced, has caused more hardship for these women.[8] Therefore, when al-Faysal exercised that right, challenging certain Jordanian "Islamic law" procedures, she caused an up-roar in the Jordanian Parliament, and some Parliament members called for her resignation, accusing her of apostasy.[9]

How could al-Hibri expect to change the patriarchal view of Islamic law—her professional venue—when she does not recognize the shortcom-ings of such solutions and interpretations despite their apparent validity? The uproar in the Jordanian Parliament was due not only to the political circumstances of the time, but also due to al-Faysal's attempt to connect the personal and the political without changing the social customary struc-ture (the *'urf*) or the perceptual views. As I described earlier, Al-Faysal's story represents an example of attempting to change the practice based on prior interpretations, without checking their theoretical validity with the Qur'anic principle of autonomous morality.

Whether or not al-Hibri was familiar with 'A'isha 'Abd al-Rahman's assertions, "Also, it is about time that men understood that their legal (*shar'i*) right to have *qawamah* over us [women], is not absolute, but is conditioned by 'what God has bestowed over some and not the other'" (Abd al-Rahman 1967, 12), such assertions add other evidence to my argument—that these female thinkers have not read the Qur'an perceptually, as Fazlur Rahman (1982) suggests. Perhaps that is because they were limited by their professional disciplinary views, by the social limitation, by the rush to prove to non-Muslim feminists that Islam is on the side of women's human rights, or by the confusion between Islamic legal law and Qur'anic law, as Maysam al Faruqi (2000) explains. 'Abd al-Rahman applied the word *ba'd* only to males, even though the verse does not specify that. Similarly, al-Hibri later made the same interpretation, as we saw above, causing the same problem that traditional interpreters did. That is, they limited the morality of the Qur'an to some legal enactment, but when the matter becomes that of women's rights, the good will or "the moral sense of the male kindness and gentleness with the 'weak rib'" is invoked, because the male has the guardianship over the female morality or financial well-being!

What else makes such scholars succumb to this interpretation of complementarities but their unwillingness to question the prevailing social structure, or their inability to self-identify with the Qur'an in a pedagogical sense (where they could develop the capacity for autonomous intentionality and authenticity) that would make explicit the principle of the Qur'anic social revolution? If the Qur'anic social revolution involving gender is to be practiced, the Qur'anic assertion that the female is an autonomous moral being who has a direct relationship with God as her only Guardian may not be compromised. Rather, it should be asserted, even if it results in a controversy.

The Muslim Woman as a Discourse

As discussions of Muslim women expand beyond the borders of the Middle East and beyond human rights advocacy, we need to collectively explore a shift in views—theoretically, methodologically, and practically—before anyone attempts to establish yet another separate field in the study of Muslims—"Muslim women's studies." The danger of establishing such a field stems not only from the crisis in social sciences (Barazangi 2001) or feminist theories (Allen 1997), or to the static understanding of Islam that resulted from Orientalist and Muslim orthodoxy, but also to creation of a new field of "Islamic studies" outside the Islamic propositions. The danger also lies in the false assumption that change is taking place merely by placing Muslim women under the microscope of social sciences, or because some Muslim women are acquiring higher academic degrees in education or positions in the labor force, and are even writing about Muslim women's issues. The underlying idea of this chapter, and my book in general, is not only to lead to the outcome, a curricular framework of "Self-Learning of Islam" (S-LI) (see chapter 5), and to debate the different perspectives (including the one proposed here), but also to engage the readers in questioning that which is taken for granted as well as deconstructing the conventional, theoretical, and methodological approaches (whether those of the secularists or the traditional religious) to the study of Muslim women, Islam, and women's issues in general.

My goal here is to go beyond critiquing these approaches and reconstructing new views—as was done, for example, in Fazlur Rahman's *Islam and Modernity*, Arkoun's *Rethinking Islam*, Shahrur's *Nahwa Usul Jadidah lil al-Fiqh al-Islami*—and also beyond the extension of the modern hermeneutics to the Qur'an discussed in the context of patriarchy and governance—as in 'A'isha Abd al-Rahman's *Al-Tafsir al-Bayani lil Qur'an al-Karim*, Mernissi's *Women and Islam: An Historical and Theological Enquiry*, Amina Wadud's *Qur'an and Woman*, and Azizah al-Hibri's "Islamic Constitutionalism and the Concept of Democracy"—and to begin constructing a dynamic pedagogical view.

The goal of this pedagogical view is not to debate "Islamic feminism" or the secular perspectives concerning Muslim women. Rather, we need to establish an understanding of the Muslim woman's concerns and realities in the Qur'anic framework, taking into consideration contemporary globalization movements, without necessarily being limited by traditionalist criteria for interpretation, or by the methodology of contemporary social science and humanities positivists or deconstructivists. I and other Muslim women scholar-activists aim to generate participatory guidelines for a policy-oriented scholarship by shifting the practice of Islamic jurisprudence as limited to the male elite and their consensus, for instance, into a community-based consultative practice, in line with the Qur'anic mandates and with Rahman's repeated assertion that the Qur'an is not a legal document. Rather, "A central aim of the Qur'an is to establish a viable social order on earth that will be just and ethically based" (Rahman 1980, 37). As participants, Muslim women—and women in general—are attempting to capture their agency in the textual interpretation process. Therefore, I want to achieve a shift in view wherein the women's participation becomes necessary not only to discuss women's and gender issues, but also as a vital contributor to Islamic morality of freedom and responsibility, seen in a fresh pedagogical and ethical dynamic. By understanding the

Qur'anic social reform pedagogically, woman's participation in the juris-prudence process will also contribute an action-based understanding of the Qur'an's gender revolution, integrating other contemporary global and cultural studies and policy-making initiatives. She will also affirm her autonomous morality as much as the moral injunctions over legal enactment.

In preparation for the self-learning curriculum, I address here the following questions:

1. How is it possible to produce an action-oriented view, using one's personal experience and professional constraints to move beyond these demarcations into comprehensive, harmonious discourses and solutions?

2. How could we argue against the present dichotomized theoretical and methodological approaches for studying the Muslim woman, be it within or outside the feminist perspectives of social sciences and the humanities? How is it possible to generate arguments outside the conventional dogmatic dichotomy of the secular and the religious, or the patriarchal and the feminist?

3. What are the premises of this view? That is, how would the central elements of this view be redressed within the contemporary contexts that will make these elements ontologically viable? How would we readjust the philosophy of knowledge about women to become universally understood and epistemologically coherent? Would we still need to use the traditional theological argumentative/hypothetical means as the methodology? How could we make our view teachable and learnable? What public-policy arguments might we generate that would be consistent with the ethics of such a view?

Tension of Self-Identity versus Complementarity's Claim

My findings among both North American and Syrian women, and about the Prophet's wives, discussed in chapters 1, 2, and 3, indicate that a higher level of formal, secular, or religious education does not correlate with Islamic higher learning. Instead, it correlates with a widening gap between male and female understanding of Islam. Muslim men tend to see Islam as something that gives them superior power and knowledge over others, despite their definition of Islam as "submission to the will of God," whereas women see Islam as a protective power by being totally submissive to the will of God as interpreted predominantly by men. In addition, higher academic education (both religious and secular) has not changed the problematic attitude about the female role in Muslim societies. Muslim women are still viewed and view themselves, in general, not as a primary principal in the familial and social relations and as having an autonomous trusteeship in line with the Qur'anic intention of *khilafah* (2:30), but only as mothers, daughters, sisters, and wives.

It is in such secondary roles that the wives of the Prophet and early Muslim women were gradually idealized by Muslim societies. The emphasis on the Prophet's wives' role as *Ummahat al-Mu'minin* (Mothers of the Believers), although carrying a level of respect and sanctity, has been the predominant representation of these pioneer Muslim women and all Muslim women. This emphasis, as we saw in chapter 3, resulted in the interpretation of the verse advising the believers to speak with the Prophet's wives from behind a curtain (*hijab*), as a generalized mandate for the seclusion of all women. It is true that the Qur'an's reference to the Prophet's wives as the Mothers of the Believers indicates two meanings: that no one may marry them after the death of the Prophet, and that they are, to the believers, the same as their own mothers (33:6), but the Prophet's wives and early Muslim women may have also played other roles in the early Muslim community that are hardly recognized.

To complicate the matter further, in today's practice, any Muslim who departs from this predominant representation of the wives of the Prophet—the complementary role—not only creates tension but also puts his or her credibility as a Muslim in jeopardy. Furthermore, it is often stated, in the course of arguments for the complementarities role, that Allah gave the Prophet's wives the choice between being obedient to him (the Prophet) in order to win paradise and the title of Ummahat al-Mu'minin, or departing from his household and losing both honors. Those who use this argument forget that the basic principle in this verse (33:28–29) is that the Qur'an gave the Prophet's wives the *conscientious moral choice*. It was a conscientious moral choice that these pioneer women made, not only because of the Prophet's outstanding moral character and their love for him and for being in his household, but also because they valued and accepted the message that he was carrying, namely, the moral choice as the base for Islamic justice, especially for women.

Our contemporary resistance to the idea of a woman being obedient to her husband—a rightful resistance, especially when it is a blind obedience and when it is perceived as the condition for partnership in marriage—should not blind us from understanding that these early women were attempting to change—in practice—the view of the time. By choosing to remain with the Prophet, by following his message and being part of his household, they seem to have done so because he was the messenger of the new view in human relations: the conscientious moral choice for each individual. Thus, these women affirmed their right to choose the new view. This is evident in 'A'isha's response to the Prophet when he read to her the above verses (33:28–29), suggesting that she might want to consult with her parents before making a decision as to whether or not to remain in his household. Her response was summarized as: "Why should I consult my parents, I want God, the messenger, and the Hereafter" (hadith 837, in the Book of Talaq in *Al-Bayan* 1998).

Therefore, as educators in Islam, how is it possible to teach that Islam requires that the Prophet's wives be blindly obedient? Are they not allowed to understand the signs of the Qur'an, and venture to disagree with the Prophet—something of which we have ample record? Are we to accept the commentaries, the books of Hadith, and history books over the Qur'anic injunctions?[10]

History books emphasize the role of 'A'isha (who is credited by al-Suyuti as second only to Abu Huraira by narrating more than two thousand hadiths) and the Prophet's wives as *muhaddithat* (narrators of the Prophet's extrapolation and practice of Islam). This view does not give a full picture of these women, though, nor does it serve as a complete practical model for Muslim women. The historical documents do not indicate that the Prophet's wives played the major role of *mufassirat* (interpreters) of the Qur'an. Although there are scattered narratives about their involvement, there is no account of their interpretation of the Qur'an, probably because they were not afforded the same learned status as their contemporary male cohorts.

In the Islamic worldview, deciphering and internalizing the signs (*ayat*) of creation in the Qur'an is, as Schimmel (1994, 114) and Rahman (1980, 1) assert, something that is endowed in human existence: "And we should show them our signs in the horizons and in themselves" (Qur'an, 41:53). What might have prevented the Prophet's wives from deciphering the sacred, in my view, is the fact that they accepted the Prophet as the ultimate interpreter of the time. The mere narratives in history books about the Prophet's wives' rivalries and attempts to protest some of the Prophet's domestic policies do not represent their autonomous interpretation of the text. Even if we Muslims accept that the Prophet was the ultimate interpreter—and we obviously do by accepting his extrapolation as the ideal for practicing Islam—his wives, as all other early Muslims, were required by their mere acceptance of the Qur'anic principle of *khilafah* to learn the revealed verses, to understand them (decipher their meaning), and then apply them autonomously. Why, then, should we assume that the Prophet's wives, early women, and all women should give up this responsibility when it is basic to Islamic principle and practice of *taklif* (obligation): if there is no knowledge and no choice, there is no obligation.

What prevented Muslim women from deciphering the Qur'an in the last few centuries, in addition to the claim of complementarities, was the introduction of the Christian and Muslim missionaries' perception that the act of deciphering the sacred required special preparation and was limited only to the elite males. When I was, for example, trying to derive the meaning of *taqwa* from my interviewees both in North America and Syria, I asked them to tell me how they could be both pious with relation to God—"piety" is the oversimplified translation of *taqwa*—and to other humans and the wombs (according to verse 4:1). A twenty-one-year-old female college student said: "As women, our first role is to attend to the family, and hence our piety to God is only possible when we pray and fast, while our piety to others is shown by accepting and fulfilling our role." Clearly, she had accepted a view of piety that showed a heavy male bias, and resulted in gendered meaning of the term. This biased meaning, it seems, has led to the injustice committed against women when they were denied the direct role of *khilafah*, and the ability to play their own moral role. *Taqwa* in Islam is the only criterion of distinction between individuals (Qur'an, 49:13). It is this criterion, set by God, by which an individual is judged when he or she strives to maintain balance of the guidance of the Qur'an, and the conscientious ethical limits of the individual with the social norms. The ability to play one's own moral role and to be freely willing to strive for this balance is what makes the conscientious moral choice to accept or reject the trusteeship meaningful.

This conscientious emancipation of Muslim women (and men) needs to be approached from a direction of education other than the merely utilitarian one. We need to approach Islamic education as the process that leads to perceptual and attitudinal change. The implications of the statement made by the young college student above extend far beyond a mere mistranslating of the Arabic word *taqwa*: This woman assumes that she can only be pious or conscious of God's presence when she performs the religious rituals, whereas Islam intends the conscientious realization that "the standard whereby [human] action is to be judged, lies outside of [human]" (Rahman 1980, 29). Furthermore, her statement implies that to be pious is to be silent, while Islam affirms that to be silent when injustice is taking place means to be impious (Qur'an, 5:9). A further implication of her statement is that to be silent is a woman's sign of consent to a marriage or any other matter that a male in her household may insist on, whereas Islam explicitly affirms that a marriage contract with the conscientious consent of both parties (orally, or by written signature) is a condition for the consummation of the marriage (Qur'an, 4:24). Such a realization makes *taqwa* or individual conscientious choice as central to Islamic identity as love is to Christian identity and law is to Jewish identity, when one speaks of the human response to the ultimate reality, the merciful justice.

Educational, historical, anthropological, and sociological studies of Muslim women rarely show interest in a relationship of spiritual and intellectual autonomous development that has more far-reaching meaning in Muslim women's struggles for justice than mere "equality" in education. Even recent studies in human rights and their implementation among Muslim women have little to do with the women's own realization of their role in understanding the Islamic belief and social system. Before introducing the Muslim woman to other concepts outside the sphere of her beliefs, such a realization is critical to effecting real and participatory change. Without realizing that her own perception of her role is in contradiction to the system that she sees as "Islam," the Muslim woman's changing of her role by another outside discourse will only bring a temporary solution.

For example, although the concept of *hawa* (Eve/woman, with a hard *H*), does not exist in the Qur'an, it is nevertheless used in the same manner as the Christian and Jewish traditional understanding as "created from the rib of Adam." Also, how could it have been possible to change the Arab/Muslim perception of women when the concept and practice of slave ownership was not abolished, nor changed even among the early Muslim leaders, despite the Qur'anic injunctions strongly encouraging setting slaves free? The story of the literate slave with the name "Hawa" (with a soft *H*) who had memorized the Qur'an and who was given as a gift by the first Umayyad caliph, Muawiyah, to Hussein Ibn Ali Bin Abi Talib (the grandson of the Prophet), is evidence of how such attitudes still prevail.[11] Even though Kahhalah (1959–1982), who brought such narration to light in his multivolume *A'lam al-Nis'* (the Who's Who among Women), might have intended to list the story of Hawa as an example of the learned Muslim women (*'alimat*), even the slaves among them, I cannot, given the Qur'anic view of conscientious moral choice, accept this rationale. That is, what kind of an example is provided by a woman who has memorized the Qur'an when she was still being treated as slave by the same Muslim leaders who were propagating Islam as a religion of moral choice and *taqwa*?

Similarly, there is no hope for change in Muslim women's role as long as the present discourses on Muslim women's emancipation still view these women as changing their role solely through the practice of wearing or not wearing special attire (*jilbab*) or head coverings (wrongly known as *hijab*) (see chapter 3),[12] and by stamping the practice of wearing special attire either as enslavement (in Mernissi's and Sa'dawi's views) or as liberating.[13] Such discourses will not change images or attitudes—by others or by Muslim women themselves—toward their identity and their role. Understanding the Muslim woman's religiosity beyond the limited discussion of her attire is basic to changing perceptions about Islamic views of the Creation and trusteeship, of morality and modesty, and of equality and equilibrium. Exploring these concepts, beginning with the Qur'an and ending with its political proponents and adversaries, is also an educational process aimed at restoring justice to the Muslim woman. Regardless of the language in which the discussion of Muslim women has been conducted, and despite the thousands of interpretations and analyses that this subject has received, the intent of the present view is to bring the discussion back to its Qur'anic pedagogical context. This intent was expressed by presenting the related verses in the Qur'an within the context of the Qur'anic chapters, synthesizing the elements of contradiction and confusion that have surrounded the discussion from the time of early interpretations to the present use of the subject (of women) for wars between groups and cultures. The goal is to propose a new meaning and a different discourse to be employed in analyzing the relationship of woman's education to her self-identity with the Qur'an and with Islam.

Self-Identity and Self-Learning
A Shift in Curriculum Development

I have used the Qur'anic pedagogical dynamics as the philosophical grounding for the Muslim woman's project to develop an integrative curriculum.[1] This curriculum proposes a shift in viewing learning, knowing, teaching, and application of the Islamic worldview, in short, living Islam. It places the learner at the center of the curricular process and the Qur'anic dynamics as the medium of the curricular design; its goal is to open possibilities for learners away from the *muqallidun* (followers of precedence) and some Orientalist focus on rituals or perceived history (structure or form), and from the present dichotomies between ideals and practice. Consequently, the learner will move in conception and practice toward the intended gender revolution of the Qur'an. In addition, she (or he) will be able to balance the tensions of pluralism and secularism.

These tensions and dichotomies have historically played major roles in the response of Muslim communities toward external knowledge and, consequently, in designing curricular and instructional material on Islam: innovation (*bida'*) versus following of precedence (*taqlid*), revelation knowledge (*naqli*) versus human-made knowledge (*'aqli*), learner's latitude for individual reasoning (*ijtihad*) versus mentor's lockstep expectations (*itta'at al-'ulama*), and modern techniques (*tajdid*) versus traditional strategies (*ta'asil*). I have considered these tensions and other issues related to self-learning of Islam and have grouped them under the seven determinants of Islamic curriculum discussed below. The goal of this long-range project is to find ways in which Qur'anic dynamics settings may aid learners in consciously resolving these tensions and issues. In this chapter, I explain how these dynamics may aid learners' acquisition and transfer of higher-order internalization of Islamic principles, or enhance a conscious, balanced process of learning, knowing, and living Islam in a particular social context (*taqwa*).

Another goal of this project is to find ways in which Qur'anic dynamics may aid learners, instructors, researchers, curriculum developers, and knowledge-base builders in formulating and implementing a new view for an integrative curriculum in Islam.[2] Self-Learning of Islam (S-LI) is a framework for a comprehensive curriculum serving as the foundation of, and the means to self-identify with, the Qur'an for a Muslim woman (or a man). Whether through a computerized World Wide Web communicative interaction or through an historical analysis, the curricular framework is intended to facilitate metacognitive learning or a higher-order thinking of Islam and of Islam's strategies for learning, knowing, teaching, and living.

The first objective of this framework is for educators to understand aspects of the learner's strategy and rationalization systems as central to the learning process. The learner's awareness of her own perceptual (ideals and practice) patterns and the transformation of her strategies are assumed to facilitate her integration of practices (procedural knowledge) and ideals (declarative knowledge) of Islam.[3] Empirical research findings suggest that prior practices and learning patterns have a negative effect on the learner's awareness of her or his own learning and on learning in the Islamic framework. Self-identity, to the contrary, facilitates conscientious relations between ideals and practice and integrated knowledge, and, consequently, transforms conceptual meanings and attitudinal and social relations.

I recognize that cases and applications do not capture what Clancey (1997, 3) calls the "situational knowledge or cognition." This is why I am proposing a shift in Islamic learning and teaching from those of the predominant *muqallidun* and some Orientalists, and from the contemporary segregated learning of religious versus secular (Qutb 1981) or of male versus female education (Ahmad and Sajjad 1984). In my view of Islamic learning, I maintain interest, as Clancey suggests, in the "collection of facts and rules in an [authentic] system" and capture the "full flexibility of how perceptions, actions, and memory are related in the brain" by understanding the individual learner's cognitive and moral processes. I call this collective, integrated process a metacognitive learning, or Islamic higher learning. This process moves with the learner beyond the behaviorists' stimulus-response process that relies on teaching "facts," and the *muqallidun* process that relies on memorization and role modeling. The teaching-learning process also moves from focusing on a learner's socially "acceptable" versus "unacceptable" performance. Instead, my focus is on the level of the learner's understanding of the concepts behind the principles as they are processed in the Islamic knowledge base (the ideals as presented in the Qur'an), and the learner's ability to integrate such concepts while deploying the principles (practical, procedural knowledge) in different contexts and within the religious-moral-rational framework.

The learning structure in this curricular framework design combines some principles of Islamic views on human learning and gender justice with contemporary theories of learning, education, and feminist studies. Although they provide an interaction-centered structure, available learning frameworks alone do not allow for learners' cognitive-moral interaction because they rely largely on predetermined assumptions and purely factual consequences. This integrative Islamic curricular framework, on the other hand, requires careful philosophical, theoretical, and methodological analyses (as outlined in my essay "The Equilibrium of Islamic Education: Has Muslim Women's Education Preserved the Religion?" 1998b). Similarly, although feminist frameworks were planned to meet certain goals in the particular social structure (Arnot 1993), they were confined by the social constraints of the time and by thoughts of sex differences and perceptions available at the time (Middleton 1993), as well as by scholars' interest in certain philosophical and theoretical aspects of the target subject.

Conversely, although religious/Muslim education furnishes knowledge-centered structures, it does not allow learners to provide perceptual input. Rahman (1980) and Schimmel (1994, 114) explain, for example, how the interpretation and use of recitation and aural/oral transfer of knowledge in an interactive action-oriented practice of Islam (before the *madrasah* system) helped to give Islam a more learner-centered worldview.[4] Just as recent innovations, such as computer tracking and tools for reflective analysis, have helped learners internalize the relationship between their patterns in the use of the program, and have given both learners and researchers a greater insight into the electronic linking of hypermedia (Barazangi 1998c; Mazur 1993, 9), the process of *ijtihad* helped early Muslim learners internalize and act on the new principles. Arkoun (1993, 106) defines *ijtihad* as the search for the basis of ontology and epistemology in order to justify Islamic rules. *Thus,* ijtihad *is a practice for each believer who faces the Qur'anic text.* When Islamic concepts are explicitly stated, Qur'anic text can become more than a subject to be committed to memory or a collection of rituals. Analyzing knowledge at several levels is necessary to achieve full understanding of a domain of knowledge embodied in a belief system (Gay and Mazur 1989, 119) just as much as self-identity is necessary to achieve the full dynamics of the Qur'an.

I will introduce this research-based curricular framework development project and explain the seven determinants that underline the evolution of the integrative curriculum.[5] The first application of this curricular framework is the interactive "S-LI" through which learners act on the internalized meaning as they integrate meaning with policy-making process. Next, I describe the Islamic belief system, whose human conception and behavior are pedagogically based on the natural human endowment as the trustee, and how the S-LI helps the learner to integrate ideals and practical knowledge.

Since the learner is the center of the curricular process, I discuss how the S-LI framework allows for interfacing with feminist or other egalitarian views, as well as for accessing other culturally based educational material (texts, media). More importantly, I explain how insights from the empirical research with S-LI learners were incorporated into the design. I conclude with some findings and their pedagogical implications, which should help us understand the relationship between prior (formulative) learning patterns and perceptual learning strategies, as well as the actual learning of Islam as perceived by learners.

Integrative Curriculum

My first task as a researcher and curricular designer in Islamic and Arabic studies within the multicultural multireligious setting of North America is to respond to the debate of pluralism, secularism, and the preservation of the individual beliefs within a seemingly secular educational system in the United States and Canada. Although Banks's (1993) definition of multicultural education as an education for life in a free and democratic society is valid for Muslims, as it is for any other cultural group, its application remains questionable. It is particularly questionable when we examine the extent to which some individuals within the Muslim cultural group take advantage of "freedom" and democracy. I define freedom as freeing oneself from passion and desires, which consequently leads to freedom from fear of mortal beings (Barazangi 1991a, 164). This is different from Morris's (1979) definition: freedom from constraints and conventions that she sees as freedom from a belief system. It is true that what secularists projected might have been a freedom from Christianity, as Hollinger (1996) suggests; yet, it certainly did not free U.S. and Canadian public education from religion. Not only are such concepts sometimes misunderstood and viewed with suspicion, but they are also used to perpetuate individual biased views and practices in what I call a "reversed multiculturalism," whether by Muslims or non-Muslims. I must caution here against considering such individual acts as sufficient excuse to consider curbing group identity, as suggested by Okin (1998). Although the possibility of reversed multiculturalism is more pronounced when issues concerning women are at stake, and consequently we may find ourselves witnessing a "reversed feminism," that does not warrant the suspicion that Okin propagates when she asks whether multiculturalism is bad for women.

Educators, therefore, not only need to be alert to a third dimension in the macro- and microcultural interaction, as Waugh, Abu-Laban, and Qureshi (1991, xii–xiv) argue, but of a fourth and sometimes fifth dimension. In their work, they present three domains in which American Muslims function: the beliefs of Islam, the individual understanding of the Muslim family, and the national domain that distinguishes the American society from others. I should add that the problem lies not in the multiplicity of these domains but mainly in the confusion between them, particularly when issues of multiculturalism are addressed using the ethnic additive approach indiscriminately. The warning of Banks (1993) against "addition of content, concepts, themes, and perspectives to the curriculum without changing its basic structure, purpose, and characteristics" is twice as important in this context. That is, the first domain, the universal beliefs of Islam that are rooted in the Qur'an, is often confused with the second domain, the individual cultural and ethnic interpretations of these beliefs, especially because these interpretations are predominantly exercised by males. Another example of confusion between such domains is the confusion between the practice of these beliefs and their principles vis-à-vis their interpretation by and within the nationalistic culture of the society at large.

My double warning applies specifically when we find that such concepts and contents are taken from secondary sources without checking the basis of the propagated perspectives, or the rationales used by their proponents as "authentic" representation of the group identity. This situation is exemplified in Okin's discussion of the North African immigrants to France. Not having examined the Islamic stance concerning head cover and polygyny at its primary sources, Okin makes assumptions without questioning whether the related practices of North African immigrants are condoned by Islam and are intrinsic to the "group identity" of Islam. That both practices were either condemned or condoned by the French government is by itself an indication that neither the government nor the author (Okin) carefully checked their sources. The French government secretly condoned the practice of polygyny among North Africans to secure more cheap labor—despite the fact that North Africans were rarely practicing it in their own country of origin—while it was opposing their practice of covering the heads of their daughters, citing secularism and liberty. Yet, when the government started facing increasingly vocal economic demands from the multiple wives and their children, and when the French economy was no longer in need of cheap labor, the government opened up the issue of polygyny and started restricting its practice. As the wives from polygynous marriages and their children were forced to go on welfare after the government refused to acknowledge their status as legitimate spouses and children, the discussion was switched to that of the danger of multiculturalism. How immoral both sides of the debate have been! What kind of morality, Islamic or otherwise, are the children of these immigrants being taught?[6]

Similarly, Nord (1995) and others began to argue that modern education is intended to secularize the Western society only when another minority religious group, especially Muslims, has become vocal. One needs only to see the explosion of literature on religion and education in the last decade of the twentieth century and Nord's subtitle, "Re-thinking a National Dilemma," to realize that the U.S. education system was not secularized but dichotomized, privatized, or made limited to schooling functions. It might have been modernized, "de-Christianized" as Hollinger (1996) points out, but religion is still the foundation philosophy of education because religion has been part of the education process since the establishment of public schools in 1647 (Mayo-Jeffries 1994, ix). Perhaps the manifestations of this philosophy and the standards by which educational ethics are being measured have varied in order that policy makers in the education system could pretend that minority groups' demands are met.

My second task, as an integrative curriculum developer from within the Islamic perspective, is to maintain a level of research standards that are based on the Euro-American modernized views of life and education, but within a worldview that is embedded in the Qur'anic view of reality, in order to make this view [of the Qur'an] accessible to the readers who are unfamiliar with basic Islamic philosophy. That is, in order to move the discussion of Islamic education into the area of Banks's (1993) third and fourth approaches, I need to change both the basic assumptions of the liberal education curriculum, using the transformative approach, and the manner by which students are involved in the decision-making and social action. Obviously, such a discussion requires another chapter, but it is critical that we here realize that the thesis of the present chapter lies both within and beyond these approaches. Without involvement in the decision-making and social-action processes, neither Islamic nor multicultural education of Muslim girls (or boys) may take place. The decision-making and social action are prerequisites for a Muslim to fulfill the article of faith and to pedagogically realize the Islamic philosophy of education, as much as they are prerequisites for helping learners acquire a sense of political efficacy.

My third task is to design an integrative curriculum for a subject matter that is rooted in the principles of inseparability of human belief, morality, and knowledge—the Islamic view as stated in the Qur'anic and other scriptural messages. This integrative curriculum poses questions vital to the present education of Muslim girls, even though it is itself neither limited to the education of Muslim woman nor to Muslims. Given that the curriculum's first condition for constructive thinking is similar to what Islam encourages—autonomy in seeing the signs of one's belief system and acting on them—does not mean that this curriculum is exclusive to females or to Muslims. Yet, the realities of teaching about, and practicing Islam, have caused Muslim girls to wonder about their own belief system. Faithful as they may be, the first question on their mind is "Why can't a Muslim woman be part of decision making?" This question becomes more critical as the women's movements become affected by trends of conservatism that are carried back and forth between the West (Europe and North America) and the majority Muslim societies. More ironic is that some of these more conservative views have traveled back from Western societies into Muslim lands during the last decade (Barazangi 1999a).

As I have explained elsewhere, the reason these girls ask such questions is their lack of direct, deep contact with the basic principles of Islam, and their inability to relate the sacred word and text to daily life. A Muslim girl who, for example, recites the verses "In the name of Allah, Guardian of the World, the Merciful, the Magnificent" (Qur'an, 1:1–2) tens of times in daily prayers without relating to their significance as defining the human relationship to God, to others, and to nature may not be able to realize herself as a Muslim (Barazangi 1997). I further argue that because women were prevented from direct involvement in Qur'anic sciences—mainly in the interpretation of the text—they are in effect not practicing Islam as the pedagogical system of trusteeship.

By discussing the Islamic system of trusteeship, I intend to focus on the importance of relating between two domains in the pedagogy of moral judgment and religious education, particularly in "pluralistic" societies like the United States: the ontological domain (the beliefs about the nature of reality), and the intellectual domain (the causal and associational standards by which we investigate reality). This relation between the two domains is rarely discussed in contemporary educational debates (for example, views on reason and revelation in Baier 1997, 65–76) and are almost absent from the discussion among American Muslim educators. Central, perhaps, to this absence is the general Muslim perception that by a mere literal imitation of the Prophet's behavior (role-modeling teaching and learning) as documented in literature, they would impart "the best of character" onto their children regardless of time and place.

A multicultural, pluralistic curriculum that develops the integrated, constructive, equilibrated, balanced (*muttaqi*) character in the learner is a rigorous and time-consuming process of conceptual and attitudinal change for researchers, instructors, students, and parents alike. But as long as such a curriculum claims to utilize pluralism with secularism as the only value base, the above visions may not be completely fulfilled. Similarly, as long as Muslim educators equate "Islamic" character with women's morality as a proxy to that of the males in her household, the human trusteeship may not be fulfilled, nor would Islamic pedagogy be actualized. Realizing the absence of deeper understanding of pluralism and secularism, including the religious philosophical foundations (see Nord's [1995, 15] argument for understanding the absence of religion from modern American education) and the secular humanistic view of curriculum development, is critical to educating and learning in the multireligious, multiethnic setting. Nonetheless, recently and more frequently, we are faced with problems resulting from the use or misuse of pluralism and its concomitant principle, individual right to freedom of expression.[7] These problems call for deeper synthesis of the concepts of pluralism, as well as of egalitarian, secular education and of religious education.

Seven Determinants of the Integrative Curriculum

The Self-Learning of Islam (S-LI) curricular framework is designed to examine the interactivity of seven determinants in the field of learning Islam, as some American Muslim learners become aware of their own meta-cognition of Islam. These determinants are as follows.

Pluralism: The Private and Public Domains

Pluralism has been implicitly taught as the value gained by the political ideology represented in the separation of public affairs from the particular, "private" belief system of a group or individuals who share one belief system (Arjomand 1993, 4). This separation is called secularism. Plurality, therefore, can in essence be understood as the antithesis of individuality or private values that govern the individual belief system and its application in both private and public affairs. The makers of the United States Constitution, we are told, thought that the means by which a pluralistic governing ideology could be established was through secularism. In other words, by taking away the right to govern from a particular religious conviction (represented at the time by the singular, theocratic institution of the church), secularity was perceived as a facilitator of the pluralistic governing body.

What actually seems to have taken place was that the individual freedom of belief and choice of a religious affiliation, which form the basis of the separation of the normative order (a private belief system) from the governing order (a public political system), was suppressed for the sake of secular plurality (see Arjomand's discussion of the relationship between religion and politics). In this context, social scientists and educators—including Muslim educators—adopted the view of society as a collection of self-regarding, independent agents but not necessarily self-regulating, morally liberated agents who behave within the Islamic principles judged only by the criterion of *taqwa*. These morally liberated agents triggered my use of the argument in Piaget's social theory (DeVries 1997) and, as William Sullivan (1982, 10–19) explains: "The liberalist themes of defense of freedom for the individual form the basis of our separation of public and private realms of discourse and activity." I should add that the secular humanist view of education and of other disciplines goes further in its demand for this separation, to the point of separation between normative and "scientific" discourses, or between human belief and knowledge, instead of separating the normative orders from their heteronymous morality represented in social egalitarianism, with a consequence of neglecting cognitive egalitarianism. That is, individuals may behave socially as though all humans were equal, and may present convincing (to the converted) evidence, but deep in their minds and hearts a dissonance thrives between their belief of the "transcendent truth" and their views of reality. This is evidenced in the repeated bigoted remarks against other religious beliefs in the plural society of America, such as the remark by Dr. Jordan, a member of the South Carolina State Board of Education described in note 7.

Arjomand expressed this situation in the context of religion, order, and pluralism as follows: "The world religions have had to face the competition not only of philosophy but also of the survivals of *pre-Axial Age* normative orders (my emphasis). These competing 'secular' normative orders progressively narrowed the sphere of religion in the course of history. This process of secularization has gone further in the West, and has resulted in considerable 'privatization' of religion. But it would be a grave mistake to assume, as is commonly done, that the pluralism of normative orders is the exclusive characteristic of the modern West." Arjomand goes on to say: "Not only do our political cultures contain both general elements and those based on culturally specific ideas of transcendence, but the public representation of the transcendent truth [as a cultural-specific feature] itself is a matter of contention within each religio-cultural tradition" (Arjomand 1993, 4).

Secularism: The Normative and Scientific Discourses

The first consequence of social egalitarianism and of the separation of the "normative" from the "scientific" is that educators ignored the fact that even scientific discourse (that is, discourses that describe, explain, or understand a phenomenon) forms a philosophical commitment that controls the way inquiry is conducted and determines the significance that the resulting knowledge will have (Shapiro, Kramer, and Hunerberg 1981, 3). A good example of this consequence is the repeated misuse of what is known as "common sense morality." Offenders seem to have lost touch with common sense morality because they have lost the thread that once held together the meanings of a moral act. By separating the normative and scientific discourses, it is more likely that one may not understand the relationship between private discourse (the spiritual, the affective, and the cognitive) and public discourse (the social and the political). As a result, the moral grounds to which individuals used to be held accountable—the ethical conduct both publicly and privately—were also lost because the relation between the public and the private was severed.

The second consequence of the separation between the normative and the scientific is that a decision maker (whether a young college student, a curriculum specialist, or a university president) is implicitly expected to forego inherent rights to freely express personal beliefs because she or he is told that this is a private discourse that underlies his or her character and philosophical commitment and has no part in the public discourse. Instead of actively dialoguing about one's own beliefs, the social pressure to decline or suppress one's views triggers, unknowingly, dissension against one's own beliefs or against the "other's" philosophical or religious convictions, especially if left untreated. This suppression often takes the form of a backlash view or policies, such as among the religious right (Gaddy, Hall, and Marzano 1996), but more damaging is the individual's projection of the "other" systems, as more recently expressed by Pat Robertson and other Christian Right leaders.[8]

The third and more damaging consequence is that the individual and private realms of discourse seem to be free on the surface through some forms of individualistic expression. Yet, in actuality, pluralistic secularists have—perhaps unknowingly—created beneath the surface a fermented conceptual conflict within the individual. This conceptual conflict, cognitive dissonance, has resulted in the majority of cases in a form of disequilibrium between the private belief system and the public political domain. Thus, what has been thought of as socially constructed minorities actually form a majority that is a socially assimilating and conceptually accommodating, but morally heteronymous, group of people. In addition, what has been thought of as majority mainstream values are socially assimilated values, exploited by some public agents instead of being a base of conflict resolution activities for cognitive egalitarianism and moral autonomy.

The overall consequence is a surge of individualism that cannot be contained by its own belief and value system. The surge of antagonistic racial, sexist, and violent irresponsible actions on school grounds and on college campuses presents more than just behavioral problems to educators. Such actions are forcing everyone to look at ethical questions as a refuge. But, unless these challenges are dealt with through the lens of deep understanding of the multicultural nature beyond social action and into the cognitive and moral autonomy (that is, the diverse views on the nature of reality and its relation to perceiving "scientific" facts) of students and teachers, all solutions will be only at best temporary.

Practical, Procedural, and Ideals Knowledge of Islam

Knowledge of Islam includes issues of Islamic fundamentals—what the Qur'an calls the "signs" (*ayat*)—of the intertwined religious and secular practices. The challenging characteristics of Islam as a belief system and the difficulties of interweaving those characteristics with the American liberal philosophy can, for example, be turned into a positive outcome instead of a dichotomous polarization between the traditional and the liberal or modern. The interwoven civil and religious character of Islam lends itself easily to the introduction of multiple representations of the principles: the ritual (prayer, individually or in mosque, mainly on a voluntary basis), civic service (voluntarism, mainly in communal gatherings), and the cultural context (a Muslim community in a Western neighborhood). Through these interactive processes, a learner may be able to understand the relationship between the religious and the civic life: on the one hand, the different forms of civic interaction and the relationship between these forms, and on the other, between these forms and the principle of praying. Once such processes are understood, the learner will be able to transfer this practical, procedural knowledge to other religious and civic functions in different social and contextual areas. Schimmel (1985, 54), for example, explains the benefit of the Prophet's recitation of Qur'anic script to purify himself for representing spiritual and meaningful instructions to his followers. Arkoun (1993, 58–59) emphasizes the importance of paying attention to the primary conditions that shaped the oral tradition [of Islam] even after it was collected and documented in written form. This attention will nurture the relationship to the logically determined meaning specific to the "writing mind" (my translation from Arabic). Arkoun adds that this attention could not be asked of Muslim jurists (*fuqaha'*) and philosophers (*'ulama al-kalam*), because their main concern is to generate rules (*qawanin*) and to protect them from outside contamination coming from thoughts other than the revelation (*wahi*). Contemporary philologists do not pay attention to the oral tradition, either.

Text Comprehension and Textual Reproduction

Reading and interpreting the text's individually reproduced and socially contextualized meanings (applying and modifying behavioral standards), and the relation between them were discussed earlier. Learners will understand and learn to apply practical, procedural knowledge of Islam as a means of communication and as a subject of social and legal changes (customs, jurisprudence, or both). Furthermore, Islam can be taught in the context of other subject areas (such as math or history). This means that learners need to understand and acquire the systemic structure and foundations of Islam, not some of their manifestations in a list of what is allowed (*halal*) and not allowed (*haram*), so as to apply them in new contexts. Thus Islamic rituals will become supportive skills, rather than the central skill to be acquired. In an Islamic course of action, integration is better than preaching about practicing; giving immediate feedback and recording civic consequences are better than diagnosing "improper behavior" and judging. By providing direct access to the Qur'anic text, learners in the Self-Learning setting focus more on the meanings and functional concepts of the principles than on memorizing the words and verses, or on external reinforcement. Stefan Wild (1996, viii) is concerned that "the Qur'anic *textus receptus,* the text as we have it, shaped and shapes the religious convictions of Muslims and is, moreover, the central cultural text in many Islamic cultures. The Qur'an is to this day for the Arabic language a supremely potent framework." Therefore, oral and scriptural aspects "have to be distinguished, but both are aspects of one and the same entity. Thus, an intertextual approach suggests itself. Moreover, the Qur'an is, in a remarkable and possibly unique way, a strongly self-referential text, a holy text with a fair share of metatextuality."

Human Knowing and Revelation Knowledge

This determinant includes issues of access to "authentic" resources, of literacy in Arabic (the language of the Qur'an), and of the history of teaching and learning Islam vis-à-vis contemporary approaches to religious/Muslim education. This kind of learning, as described also in determinant 2 above, is called conscientious learning, and is intended to signify acquisition and transfer of higher-order thinking skills and Islamic higher learning. It calls for a change in the conception of the structure and function of a learning institution, in the conception of the instructor or leader's role and behavior in the classroom or the mosque, and of the conception and planning of Islamic studies, Islamic education curriculum, and the learning outcomes. I, for example, favor the introduction of "authentic" texts (Qur'anic verses) as the base for teaching and learning Islam; by working with the authentic texts, the ritualistic and behavioral principles can be dealt with as they occur, not in the abstract. Yet, the meanings and behaviors of these principles have not been formed because of the customary knowledge and popular beliefs of the dogmatic preaching. According to Arkoun (1993, 107), these dogmatic beliefs are what shaped the ethical law and the metabehavior about history, human, and God. He adds, therefore, that *ijtihad* today will certainly shake these popular beliefs, changing habits and attitudes. Thus, it is a form of civilizational work that caused creative dynamics in Muslim thinkers of the first three centuries of Islam. It was these dynamics that resulted in intellectual and cultural production and in an epistemological system of a legal, social, and political order.

Instruction or Mentoring and Self-Learning or *Ijtihad*

This determinant includes issues of learners' latitude to manage their learning vis-à-vis teachers' tolerance to changing their role and their view of Islamic teaching. In the S-LI framework, teachers, instructors, and leaders will be promoting learning and the use of critical thinking and problem-solving skills within the Islamic worldview and the subsequent "successful" transfer of those skills to problem solving in different subject areas, applying principles and rationalization in different social contexts. Successful transfer means that learners are learning and understanding the moral and cognitive concepts underlying the problem-solving procedures (reinterpretation of text, jurisprudence, or mere personal opinion and rationalization) and can then apply those same procedures appropriately in different contexts (Mandinach 1994). Consequently, classroom, home, and mosque dynamics will also be different. Therefore, we need to visit all these fields, but with a new set of lenses in order to reproduce a collective logical theology for the liberation of all humans.

"Modern" Learning versus "Traditional" Strategies

I suggested earlier that modern learning strategies give way to integrative curricula in the Islamic framework, including functionality, effectiveness, the purpose of learning, prior learning patterns, and perceptions of religious and secular knowledge. In this context, I briefly analyze one aspect of this determinant: the effect of prior perceptions and learning patterns and how they affect the objective of integration of private and public domains, as well as the objectives of innovation versus precedence, revelation versus human-made knowledge, individual reasoning versus the authority of Islamic scholars, and modern versus traditional techniques.

Educational Objectives of the Self-Learning of Islam

In the first phase of building the S-LI framework, the program was intended for Muslim women learners to build or map their own assumptions, theories, and strategies and rationales on a personal level. Evaluation of the program by learners themselves was also incorporated into the curricular design, as an interactive reflective implementation of consciousness enhancement through the course of dialogue among participants in different study circles or electronic lists.

Learners' Needs and Interests

The general guiding principle was to develop the curricular goals and a self-assessment instrument that is neither structurally rigid nor discouraging to instructors and learners. For example, instead of proceeding with the conventional process of writing a mission statement, stating the philosophy, and then presenting the topical content (the subject of discussion), learners were presented with a topic that was closest to their interest, such as a current event, in the form of a problem or an issue that begged a solution or a discussion.

Given that one of the aims of Islamic education is "character building" to achieve the *muttaqi* (balanced) personality, I realized that I could not start with the concept of God, nor with the article of faith. Not only do these topics already represent part of the discourse of the Muslim mentor/ learner (and are often taken for granted as a set of *apropos* beliefs without which a person cannot be assumed to have accepted Islam), but Muslims have not fully translated these concepts into ethical and pedagogical dynamics, as a result of the way these concepts have been generally perceived and taught. Conceptual-change theorists, such as Strike and Posner (1983), Posner (1983), and Barazangi (1989, 1988) assume prior perceptions of a concept as a determinant in the learning of new concepts. Thus meaningful, effective learning requires a metacognitive process of reflection on one's own interpretation and practice of a particular concept. As new concepts and meanings (including new contexts and rereading of the Qur'anic text) are introduced or made directly accessible to the learners, learners reconstruct their own learning scheme (for example, prior learning patterns) and meanings (for example, new interpretation), and create new rationalization and insights. The metacognitive learning module proposes to achieve an efficient and appealing way of reconstruction and creation through the self-learning process.

That is, instead of starting with "the absolute transcendence, God" as a highly abstract and very dominating concept, one may begin with the issue of social interaction across sexes. The aim of building a *muttaqi* personality, therefore, could be achieved through the individual learner's awareness of her rationalization and by comparing the types of resources (human or otherwise) that she is exploring in order to reach an answer or a solution. Literature abounds with examples that strikingly confirm the success of the instructional framework of a project contracting with learners, for example. It is the inquisitive process that a learner goes through as part of a problem-solving task that enhances consciousness raising and self-learning, and not the nature of information or the accumulation of knowledge for the sake of knowledge only, and the solving of the problem itself.

In this framework, the instructor facilitates the learner's search for the sources, and, hence, the meaning of the "transcendent God," for example, will be integrated and learned through a keen interest in a particular topic. In this way, learning and internalization of the sources and of the material will be of higher value and have a more lasting effect. At this level of discussion, the golden rule of the instructor is not to be dogmatic. To speak of connectedness to God as the ultimate judge, for instance, may result in fear, instead of enhancing reverence or internal consciousness of God (as a source of knowledge and value). Internal consciousness by itself makes a person practice Islamic ethics. Therefore, the choice of certain meanings, particularly the meaning of "God," becomes very central to the success of the curriculum. If the goal is to develop a character of a *muttaqi*, then that person needs to understand and accept the concept of being a trustee whose character is to approximate that of God's attributes, instead of seeing herself only as being detached from and fearing God.

Another example is the general Muslim use of subservient expressions, such as "submission," and the ones evoking servitude, such as "working for the pleasure of God." These expressions are placing meanings upon Islam that do not allow for human connectedness to God. Submission has more fatalistic, negative connotations than Islam intends the relation of the human to God to be. The Qur'an intends this relation to provide a framework for the human to act within the textual guidance in order to recognize God's creation and become closer to realizing one's character in reality. Similarly, servitude is not Islamic, because God's mercy is not tied to God's pleasure—mistakenly ascribed to God as if God had different moods comparable to those of humans, or as if God needed such servitude. According to the Qur'an, God made humankind of higher nature than any other creature by giving humans the ability to conscientiously choose or to refuse being the trustee of the *amanah* (the guidance). God's guidance explains a possible final outcome for either choice. Thus, the first work of educators is to preserve this important character of what makes a human. This can happen when human relatedness to God is understood in this context of trusteeship, and cannot be realized in the context of servitude.

The Self-Learning framework also allows both mentors and learners to self-assess their own teaching or learning by the end result of their respective project or discussion. Mentors and leaders will, of course, provide check-and-balance points, or direct learners to where these may be available in the Islamic text. Mentors may also draw broad guidelines as to how to accept a source and check its validity, and as to what constitutes an "Islamic methodology" or an Islamic-oriented project. Learners will actually learn the skills of recitation and interpretation of the Qur'an, for example, as a means for conducting their search. These skills are acquired in the process of executing the project as needed, instead of being taught in isolation as a subject of study without an immediate meaningful application.

By adopting this philosophy, not only can the curriculum achieve a link between the skills learned in the society at large and the Islamic character skills, but—more importantly—a link between the two worlds of the Muslim learner will be achieved: the world of the Muslim community and that of the social environment at large. The major problem in the way Islam is being taught to children and youth, for example in North America, is— according to Susan Douglass–that there is no integration between the world history and geography that Muslim students are learning in public schools, and the experience and the information about the world that these students receive in weekend Muslim schools (personal e-mail communication, June 1999).

Learners' Interactivity

In addition to pedagogical and ethical objectives of the S-LI framework, the issues presented were intended to expose learners to two different phases in the integrative learning process. In the first phase, I incited learners to think of their rationales and strategies while discussing a particular issue during the focus group interviews. I also asked if they had used a particular strategy (such as planning or evaluating) in a different context, thus making them aware of their own prior patterns of rationalization and of such strategies. In the second phase, while reflecting on their own discussion (by responding to the transcribed tape of the focus group interview or to an electronic discussion), learners were asked whether they had applied some of the strategies that were presented earlier. Some reported that they had used some of these strategies during their study circle or when they were independently reviewing some material.

By listening and responding to the discussion, learners went through a dynamic, analytic, problem-solving procedure and reflective analysis of their own learning strategies (Oxford 1990). Based on learners' statements of interest in learning about Islam and other perceptions of the Islamic belief system, the framework was designed to further learners' input. This input, summarized in my paper (1998b) and other case studies presented in this book, will help further the development of the objectives of the S-LI framework.

The issue here is not merely whether learners know the meaning of a principle but whether they have access to Islamic ethical functionality. This access resembles that which permits the intuitiveness of the natural endowment of reason, leading learners to the determinants in the authenticity of a principle and variations in its interpretation and use. Thus, historical as well as socioanthropological aspects of religion and ethics play a role in determining the level and the nature of the content in a curricular planning of Islam. It is not only a matter of spiral difficulty or level of proficiency or practice but also of what and how much of other related knowledge one may, or can, include, and how to integrate it with learners' needs and interests as well as with cultural contexts. These latter issues could be addressed by the learners' direct access to knowledge bases of Islam, be they of the fundamental system (rituals and forms), literature, history, or any content (cultural themes or the use of Islamic principles within other curricular contexts such as social sciences), or Islamic ethical or functional-based (communicative aspects) instruction and action.

The obstacle of splitting into rhetoric and action could also be explained by the difficulties in authenticity features, such as the variation in the level of primacy of the Qur'an over the Hadith, in addition to the agency of the interpreter in her direct access to these sources. Yet, given the simplicity of the issues in the program (consisting mainly of the intermixing between the sexes or learning Arabic as the language of the Qur'an), the prior-patterns factor seems a more likely explanation (Barazangi 1991a, 1991b). The obstacle might also be attributed to learners' inability to apply the variation between Qur'an and Hadith because of the jurisprudence books or the mentor's ambiguity as to what constitutes an authentic principle. This is exemplified in the distinctive variation between the meanings loosely given to *shari'a*. There is the *Shari'a* of the Qur'an (with a capital

S) as the primary source of the ideal and the only divine, binding source, the *shari'a* of the Hadith as the primary source of extrapolating the Qur'anic principles in context and the only exemplary application, and the *shari'a* that includes these two sources and their interpretations by many jurists. This latter meaning is often thought of as binding.

Some findings from the reflective data suggest a negative effect of prior practice patterns on the learners' awareness of their own learning and on learning within the Muslim versus the Western environment. The pedagogical implications of such findings are to involve the learners in modifying the design of the program, thus increasing their awareness of the power of consciously using interactive learning strategies to make learning an internal process as much as it is an external outcome potentially evaluated for effectiveness and action.

One of the goals of this integrative curricular development process is enabling the learners to understand the aspects of their own strategy systems that will make them capable of reflection. This understanding also helps educators to assist learners in explicitly expressing these strategies and in drawing relationships to their own prior perceptual patterns. Such relationships also make learners aware of the power of consciously using learning strategies. This awareness is shown to facilitate learners' integration of practical, procedural, and ideal declarative knowledge of Islam with critical thinking and problem-solving skills and underlying Islamic foundation principles that guide their application to diverse contexts.

The Muslim Woman's Education

The goal of the Self-Learning of Islam curricular framework is to generate pedagogical guidelines for a policy-oriented scholarship by shifting the practice of Muslim jurisprudence, for instance, into a community-based consultative practice. Community-based consultation is the first principle of Qur'anic governance (Qur'an, 42:38) that would help to move the Qur'anic ideals into practice. Yet, because Muslims largely moved from the ideals into practice without developing a pedagogical theory, the consultative process became limited to the select elite males who acquired some research tools, but it did not allow for testing their hypotheses against the actual change in the social phenomenon, as Cummins (1999) suggests is happening among Western educators. The community-based consultation principle is also in line with Rahman's (1980, 37) repeated assertion that the aim of the Qur'an "is to establish a viable order on earth that will be just and ethically based." But because the principle was moved abruptly into practice, and eventually, the practice became the norm for policy making, Muslims have no developed theory to check the validity of application. Being largely absent from participating in this process, Muslim women who are trying to recapture their own agency in the textual interpretation process need to move one step further.[9] The hope is that woman's participation becomes necessary not only to discuss women's and gender issues, but also to discuss Islamic morality of freedom and responsibility in the public arena in a fresh pedagogical dynamic, achieving a shift in views. By understanding and applying the goals of the Qur'anic social reform pedagogically, the Muslim woman's participation in the jurisprudence process will not only change the legal standards but more importantly will also contribute to other contemporary global and cultural theories and policy making, affirming her autonomous morality as much as the moral and rational injunctions of the Qur'an over legal enactment.

While I was working with a number of Muslim communities, seeking an understanding of their perception of the Islamic belief system and how they are transmitting it to their children (Barazangi 1988), several factors triggered my long-term interest and research work on educating the Muslim woman with/in the pedagogical dynamics of the Qur'an.[10] This long-term research required a simultaneous exploration of the American multicultural curriculum (Barazangi 1993) and the foundations and practice of "Islamic" and Muslim education in the United States and other Muslim societies. In this section, I briefly restate these foundations, using the examples from my ethnographic data to illustrate my own shift in viewing Islamic learning and education in general.

Dualism in Education

As a result of dualism in education—secular modern versus religious traditional—introduced to Muslim societies through European colonial and missionary work, Muslim practice during the nineteenth and twentieth centuries "transformed the Qur'anic pedagogy from understanding and acting on the parameters set in the Qur'an for constructive relationships" into a list of "Islamic" versus "non-Islamic" do's and don'ts (Barazangi 1995a, 406). Compounded with males' perception of women's moral dependency—contrary to the Islamic principle of autonomous morality in which each individual is accountable for his or her own work—Muslim educators imposed certain standards of behavior for girls (for example, being bashful, wearing special customary clothing, and refraining from public interaction with the opposite sex) without requiring similar standards for boys. Thinking that they were protecting the religion by instilling the habit of "female seclusion or segregation," which also reinforced the impression that raising Muslim girls ought to be totally different from raising boys, they actually secluded the minds and souls of these girls who were the mothers and the first teachers of the future generations. Such practices were further used in an exploitative fashion against Islam, and, hence, Muslims were also stigmatized as incapable of being "rational, scientific or democratic" because they associate with Islam (Lueg 1995, 16).

Not only are U.S. Muslim communities growing in number (Ba-Yunus and Siddiqui 1998; Nu'man 1992), but their educational institutions are becoming more visible (Muhammad 1998) and often fall to the dichotomies of humanistic (assumed as rejecting the concept of God) versus religious (assumed as representing Islamic education). Complemented by, or complicated by, recent educational reform movements, especially the debates about government intervention (Bluenfeld 1995, 7) and about introducing moral and religious curriculum (Haynes 1994), Muslim educational practices may bring different perspectives into the multicultural equation but may not move toward the consultative process.

Educators such as Lickona (1997) and Alan Lockwood (1997) are directing their attention to virtue and character education, respectively. What used to be the focus in the 1970s and 1980s of moral and value clarification education in the United States took in the 1990s new forms and labels, such as "the family state, the state of families, and the state of individuals" (Guttman 1987 as quoted in Lugg 1996, 31–32). Others are investigating citizenship education. Addressing what Anne Turnbaugh Lockwood (1997) calls "troubled times," a third group is discussing religious education as either a troubling or a necessary phenomenon. Gaddy, Hall, and Marzano (1996) call their collection *School Wars: Resolving Our Conflicts over Religion and Values*. William J. Bennett (1992) talks about the fight for "our culture and our children." A fourth, similar trend is forming within the fields of history and cultural studies. Hollinger (1997, 1996) is moving the "ethno-racial diversity" debate to the "postracial, the religious" debate. Glazer (1997a) is accepting that "we are all Multiculturalists," and discusses religious conservatism and American diversity (1997b, 125–41). More recently we see the debate over charter and voucher schools replacing the debate on equity in education, as was attempted in the 1984 United States Commission on Excellence report, *A Nation at Risk: The Full Account*. In 1995 we were reading the Carnegie Council on Adolescent

Development's *Great Transitions: Preparing Adolescents for a New Century,* and in 1993, the National Governors Association report, *Ability Grouping and Tracking.* Now we are reading (mostly on the World Wide Web) the views of the New Right conservatives or the defenders of civil liberties. Yet, to my knowledge, few views of Muslim educators are indexed or expressed within the "mainstream" educational literature.[11] Why?

I argue that the major reason behind this invisibility is the low involvement, and low effectiveness, of Muslim women in the decision-making process among these communities. One reason for their low effectiveness and visibility, perpetuated across new generations of Muslims, is the general perception that women are the preservers of culture and religion by proxy.[12] Another reason for this invisibility is the denial of Americans, particularly strong in the circles of educators, of the fact that the Muslim population in the United States is close to 8 million[13] and that Muslims have different needs beyond the window-dressing, multicultural, multiethnic understanding.[14]

Transforming the Multicultural Discourse

In this book, I suggest that a transformation in the framework for investigating multiculturalism, moral, character, or religious curricula is needed if we are to observe a significant change resulting from the contemporary "educational reform" movements, particularly in Western societies such as the United States and Europe. As issues of character building and religious identity are making a visible dent both within educational assessments and religio-ethnic cultural studies, I concern myself with the cross-cultural understandings of what we mean by any type of education that takes religion, value, character, moral, or any other similar term as a subtext, especially when the woman's morality is seen as proxy to that of the males in her household.

Although the claim is often made for the need to discuss the framework of multiethnic, multireligious curricula,[15] a predominant male elite interpretation of Islam, Muslims, and Islamic education, I postulate, might have shaped the character of the young Muslim girls living in the United States and Canada. As these girls marry and take on their role as women, the perceived limits of this role are perpetuated through the next generations. While females represent the majority of practicing educators, the domination of Muslim male interpretation of "Islamic education" and decision making in more than 250 full-time "Islamic schools" in the United States[16] (and other, part-time, weekend, formal, and informal educational settings) advocate the perception that females are merely the preservers of Islamic culture and Islamic religion as interpreted by the male elite, and need different, separate education from that of males.[17] In addition, when issues of religious versus public schools are discussed, they are mainly discussed in popular Muslim culture magazines, and more recently in Web pages, and the focus is often on the female covering versus corruption by sexual promiscuity, coeducation, teenage pregnancy, and so on.[18]

Muslim parents and educators do not see the need for each individual—male or female—to translate Qur'anic principles into new practices. As the woman generally relies on interpretations of others, she is seen mainly as preserving stale applications of Islam from another context, instead of being educated to become involved in the understanding of the *Din* (worldview) in the new context. Despite their claim of a different philosophy of education—the philosophy that is rooted in the ideals of Islam—contemporary Muslim educators do not differ in their perception of female education and role modeling from the general view that the school environment is "a place where the knowledge, historical perspectives and values that are basic for our culture [in the United States] are passed from one generation to the next" (Gaddy, Hall, and Marzano 1996, xi). The difference is in the nature and content of the values, or so it seems, that each group appears to propagate.[19]

The Gender Equation

By introducing gender as a dimension of diversity along with religious values and ethnicity, I am shifting the focus to another level of religious/moral education and to another meaning of learning and construction of knowledge. I am also shifting the discussion of educating the Muslim woman from being an add-on topic to being a first priority at the center of discussing Islamic education. I propose that without making the woman's Islamic higher learning (deeper knowledge of Islamic principles and the rules of interpreting principles into action) central to issues of Islamic education, particularly in the Western context, neither "Islamic" nor any religious or moral education will make a difference in the education of Muslims.

In addition, no other change would take place in the perception of Islam, Islamic education, and of Muslim education in the "pluralistic" society in the United States, or within the "politics of identity" in the globalization process. That is, the claim of the United States and other Western societies for multicultural, multireligious education not only becomes mute, but also problematic. It has, in fact, become little more than lip service. To the *muqallidun* Muslims in those societies, multicultural education is an add-on, but they cannot see the difference between maintaining the ideals and maintaining the practice—the customary knowledge—for applying Islam in the new context (Hull 1998).

Since the goal of the Self-Learning of Islam is to achieve an equilibrium (*taqwa*) or a balance between the individual—with the ability to make choices as Islam instructs in order to live out the "trust" God has given to human beings—and society's needs, without putting limits on female Islamic higher learning, I will conclude this chapter by offering some practical strategies.

Taqwa is both a goal and a means to the balanced Islamic education (referred to in 3:110 of the Qur'an as the process of shaping one's character in a coherent Islamic worldview) within a particular context.[20] My assumption is that the Islamic principle of *taqwa* refers to human conscientious balance between individual and societal needs and is the only criterion in judging the success or failure of Islamic education, much as it is the only criterion of differentiation between individuals ("the noblest among you is the balanced one [*muttaqi*]," Qur'an, 49:13). The purpose of the Qur'an is not only to propagate a theology of God, or a philosophy of reason and revelation, as Lickona (1997) suggests, but mainly to present pedagogical guidelines for constructive human interaction with others.

A successful constructive interaction with others, therefore, calls for educators to understand the microculture, and not only to call for the ability of the microculture to provide the learner with the right skills to function effectively in his or her different cultural settings, as Banks (1993) suggests. To fulfill the purpose of human existence as the trustee, a Muslim must at least be acquainted with the Islamic system and its methodologies before she or he can turn the article of faith into action. Understanding the Islamic worldview is as simple as the ability to recite and know the meaning of the article of faith stripped of the many layers of translations and meanings that over time have added gender, class, ethnic, or other biases. This does not imply cutting off previous knowledge and heritage, nor imposing limits on acquiring the knowledge, attitudes, and skills needed to engage in public discourse, but keeping these sources in their rightful secondary place. The issue of Muslim women's Islamic higher learning, and participation in the interpretation of the texts and in decision making, is, therefore, allowing the Qur'an to speak for itself to the individual woman and to be this individual's primary guide.

Why Islamic Education?

Islamic education is giving back to boys and girls their true right, the true expression of their moral, private existence—the goals of which are intricately interrelated with the goals of the communities to which these persons belong—in a manner integrated with their public existence. As educators and policymakers we may be able to perpetuate the chance for true tolerance to grow, by allowing the reunification of the human belief system with its moral and political action. We can replace the instrumental moral and political outlook by a concern for the ethical quality of social relationships, shared initiative, and moral responsibility. To be a conscientious being both in thought and in action is to follow the natural pattern in which humans were created, the pattern in which humans actualize the Divine Will through their own will and action (Qur'an, 30:20). To the contrary, as long as we expect individuals to separate their belief from their political action, duality in action and window-dressing pluralism will prevail ever more. Through a process of understanding and application of an integrative belief and action, the practice of multicultural design will go beyond the form of aggregated private opinions into a common ground, and will be expanded to include a search for shared meanings. These shared meanings can be incorporated into the curriculum by the learners through their participation in discussing the particular issue by gathering pertinent data, analyzing their values and beliefs, synthesizing their knowledge and values, and identifying alternative courses of action (Banks 1993). Yet, the process neither starts nor stops at this level of social action. We need to move toward understanding how individuals relate between values and beliefs when making a decision about a particular course of action.

The advantage of such an integrative curriculum is that it will not take away, as the liberalist tradition did, perhaps unintentionally, the ability and the desire of the learner to deal with his or her own problems from the communities of individuals. Not even the conservatives would disregard such a curriculum as government interference in individual and local community affairs. Such a curriculum will realize the complex relations among private and public discourse in social and educational programs instead of merely gathering and using scattered techniques and information. Finally, the question of what image of human nature and society should guide our practice can be answered simply by examining our given premise and its results. By examining pluralism and its principles of secularism and individualism, we realize that they are no longer a source of an adequate moral image of human nature, such as the different interpretations of the Creation story. Thus, investigating and understanding each other's belief systems and views of reality might be the first step toward cognitive egalitarianism.

Let us, for instance, examine the premise of the need for a metaphysical belief in a multicultural, pluralistic curriculum from the Islamic point of view. In his answer to the question "Why God at all?" Fazlur Rahman (1980, 2) wrote, "The Qur'an calls this 'belief in and awareness of the unseen.' This 'unseen' has been, to a greater or lesser extent, made seen through revelation for some people like the Prophet, although it cannot be fully known to anyone except God. God's existence can, however, be brought home to those who care to reflect so that it not only ceases to be an 'irrational' or 'unreasonable' belief but becomes *'the Master-Truth'*" (Rahman's emphasis). Rahman goes on to say that "in order to achieve this, students must do something; if they do not, they cannot be called students at all. It is therefore, not an extraordinary or an unreasonable or a supererogatory demand. The student must 'listen' to what the Qur'an has to say: 'Who is humble before the unseen and brings with him [or her] a heart such that it can respond [when the truth hits it]' (50:33)."

The problem, Rahman laments, is not how to make a [hu]man come to belief by giving lengthy and intricate 'theological' proofs of God's existence, but how to shake him [or her] into belief by drawing his [her] attention to certain obvious facts and turning these facts into 'reminders' of God and their humanity. Hence, the Qur'an time and again calls itself (and also the Prophet Muhammad) 'a reminder' or 'The Reminder.'" The Qur'an, I must add, refers to all the prophets and apostles as those who possess the (reminding) message (11:7), and says that the "master truth" may not be known without intimate human knowledge (7:33).

Rahman concludes: "Once we have grasped these three points—that everything except God is contingent upon God, that God is essentially the all merciful, and that both these aspects necessarily entail a proper relationship between God and man and consequently also a proper relationship between man and man, we will have understood the absolute centrality of God in the entire system of existence, to a very large extent because the aim of the Qur'an is the man and his behavior, not God" (1980, 3). If we accept these premises, as Muslims often do, then why does the reality of a Muslim girl's education lack all these elements? The search for an answer to this question was the flame that ignited this work.

Conclusions

Where Do We Go from Here?

In this book I described how women have been affected by specific interpretations of the Qur'an, such as the reduction of the meaning of trusteeship to political and theological leadership exercised by men alone. I evaluated the heightened consciousness and the changes in public policy brought about by some American and Syrian Muslim women, and showed how some of these conventional interpretations are invalid when one reads the Qur'an pedagogically. Using the criteria expressed in the Qur'an's instruction to "read in the name of God" and in the concept of *taqwa*, I demonstrated how a pedagogical reading of the story of Creation leads to a renewed understanding of trusteeship and women's morality and modesty, as well as equality and *taqwa* from within the Qur'anic text, and I discussed some opportunities for the Muslim community to build on these meanings. By recognizing the positive contributions made by these self-identified Muslim women, we may be able to extend their contributions toward attitudinal change and toward participatory policy making based on the new meanings.

In this conclusion I would like to emphasize the central issue that still challenges not only Muslim women but also other religious scholars and practitioners: *Why has the authority to interpret "religious" texts been exclusive to male religious elites?* I would suggest that unless we recognize women as having such an authority, nothing will change. As a strategy toward this goal, I have proposed a curricular framework, "Self-Learning of Islam" (S-LI), as a means for self-realization and self-identity, that is, as a means to be Qur'anically grounded. In order to make a space for Muslim women to assume and claim this grounding and, with it, their authority as trustees in the Qur'anic sense, the following two questions, addressed under the next two subheadings, are still begging for answers and call for further action-oriented research. To change both the intellectual discourse and the realities of these women, we need to address two questions: (i) who will be the agents of charting and implementing the new meanings into policy; and (ii) when will it be possible to claim the legitimacy of the Self-Learning framework.

Charting and Implementing the New Meanings into Policy

To chart and implement the new meanings we need to first recognize the intolerance and harsh critique that earlier scholars, such as bell hooks and Middleton, received from within their own discipline, let alone accepted by the "guardians" of "academic integrity and freedom of expression." I expect to face similar uneasy treatments by both the "guardians" of the fields of Islamic studies, women's studies, and Middle East women's studies, on the one hand, and by the Muslim male elites on the other (Barazangi 1993). For instance, neither Muslim educators nor today's universities and colleges in North America are able or willing to envision the long-range goal or the in-depth self-assessment in which students in a self-learning discourse will have to engage.[1] Perhaps they perceive such a goal to be a threat and, therefore, resent it. Such resentment might be caused by a certain fear of actually changing the learners' ability to assess themselves and their own prior knowledge of the subjects, or worse, the fact that these learners might question the "authority" in their respective disciplines.[2] It is small wonder then that the focus in academia is still on the distribution requirement while diversity is relegated to the human resources administration. Meanwhile, interdisciplinary programs, such as women's studies, are being uncritically assimilated into the academic mainstream while their discourses are being co-opted within the traditional views of the professional disciplines (Greenwood 2004; Barazangi 2001).

Similarly, the *muqallidun* (followers of precedent) Muslim elites not only fear the questioning of their authority but fear that women might take over the leadership initiatives if they were allowed to change the meanings and the discourse and engage in the reinterpretation of the Qur'an. As a Muslim and as an academic feminist action researcher affiliated with Cornell University Women's Studies Program (in the fall of 2002 the name was changed to Feminist, Gender, and Sexuality Studies, another phenomenon that needs analysis, but in another book), I have been searching for answers to this general research question: If the Qur'an, the primary reader of Islam, is intended to dismantle hierarchies and social heteronomy/hegemony and to enact social justice, including gender justice, how then could the discussion concerning the status of Muslim women become so polarized in the first place? And why has the Muslim woman herself, until recently, been so absent from this discussion?

In general, Muslim women accept the Islamic worldview as rational and just, yet their social realities are evidence to the contrary. The social realities of Muslim women strikingly contradict the ideals of Islam and could be considered oppressive. Muslim women not only have the highest illiteracy rate and the highest infant mortality rate (*The World Almanac and Book of Facts*, 2004), for example, they also have been excluded from policy making even at the level of local governing boards. Yet, to focus on these realities as the problem, as many feminists do, instead of understanding them as behavioral manifestations that result partly from colonialism and are mainly due to male-biased interpretations, does not support Muslim women's self-identity with Islam as a means to achieve social justice. Furthermore, by attributing these realities to Islam, non-Muslim or Westernized Muslim feminists have caused a defensive attitude among Muslim women and often a rejection of feminism. Meanwhile, Muslim male elites who wrongly attribute the exclusion of women from public participation to the Qur'an have caused women not to be empowered with Qur'anic tools of liberation and have kept them from living out their trusteeship. At times, Muslim women have experienced a tension of contradictions in their identification with Islam because they were erroneously made to believe that males' interpretations were as binding as the Qur'anic principles themselves.

As suggested earlier (Barazangi 1998b), the polarized interpretations of the status of Muslim women and the resulting tensions seem to come from a combination of ideological and scholarly dichotomies between two polarized views concerning Western and traditional Muslim interpretations of Islam and gender justice. On the one hand, there is a discrepancy between community ideals and practices, according to which women are idealized as mothers, daughters, and wives but not recognized as autonomous moral and rational beings as intended in the Qur'an and extrapolated in chapter 3 of this book. On the other hand, there is a confusion of identity between the Islamic worldview—practicable only by a conscientious, Qur'anically grounded identity—and of an ethnic identity with a particular Muslim culture such as Arabic. Arabic exercises a considerable influence on the Islamic mind-set, being both the language of the Qur'an and the culture in which Islam grew (Barazangi 1991a, 1991b). In other words, in order to chart and implement the new meanings (presented in chapters 1–4 of this book) in policy, we need to move our understanding of Islam from the instrumental level into that of a critical-reflexive knowledge and understanding of the Qur'an. Furthermore, in order to ground the Islamic worldview in concrete conceptualization and practices for social justice, a Muslim needs to self-identify conscientiously with Islam as her or his primary identity. Meanwhile, the question of ethnic identity, such as one's identity as Arab, Persian, or Turkish, or one's gender identity, such as woman or man, is only secondary to being a Muslim.

Claiming the Legitimacy of Self-Learning

To claim the legitimacy of Self-Learning, we need to examine genesis of critiquing the disciplines of women's studies, women's education, and "Islamic" education. Although the three works analyzed in the first section above (Barazangi 1993; hooks 1994; Middleton 1993) were written for different cases and from different worldviews, they share the same historical context. At the time when the New Right movements were lashing out at different cultural groups, including women, and as these groups voiced their concerns about curricular inclusions and exclusions, these backlash reactions manifested themselves in multicultural versus mainstream curricula, in affirmative action admissions and testing practices, and in social welfare policies.

The contemporary context adds emphases by funding agencies on educational components in research proposals even by the National Science Foundation, especially in grades K–12. Residential learning among college students is assumed to replace or complement ethnic-based dorms or language houses with new compounds and a shift in living concentration. At the same time, the old philosophy of dichotomized subject matters and fields of study still prevails in discussions of liberal arts curricula. A recent report by the curriculum committee of the Cornell College of Arts and Sciences still classifies reasoning skills into quantitative and qualitative skills, with an "add-on" of moral reasoning and the study of ethics. Furthermore, engagement learning continues to be treated mainly as a practical skill for the arts and sciences and is not seen as part of the main mission. I should state at the outset of this section that even though I was institutionally trained as a curriculum specialist, a psycholinguist, and a cognitive scientist, and majored in philosophy and sociology in my undergraduate studies, my remarks on the legitimacy of my Self-Learning curricular framework cannot be divorced from my self-identity and self-learning with/in the action-oriented philosophy of Islamic education. I point this out in order to set the stage for understanding the interaction of identity and knowledge when designing, implementing, and evaluating a curriculum. That is to say, this discussion is not about including Islamic philosophy of education, feminist education, or ethnic studies in university curricula. It is, rather, about the "forgotten factor," that is, that which is forgotten when mapping the successes and failures of the social sciences and the humanities curricula or, for that matter, any other curriculum. And what is that forgotten factor? The forgotten factor is that conscious inquisitive process that a learner goes through as she or he attempts to make sense of and to act on the nature of knowledge, its origin, and evolution, with the goal of self-realization as a citizen and as a moral being.

Beginning with the selection of reading material for the new course of study, Middleton states, one would still have to prepare one's teaching in a conventionally "academic" manner—whatever that may mean—and yet, at the same time, present the contemporary feminists' views and other concomitant views with regard to women's education and sociology of education. Such an instructor is expected to be innovative in teaching method as well as in the content of the course. She is to present feminists' views on education while using and thereby affirming, one more time, the conventional didactic, positivist means of "liberal" education and "the requirement" of the particular discipline, such as history, government, religious studies, and so on. Therefore, in 1999 I asked how such teaching could challenge the present discourse of women's education while continuing to use the traditional dogmatic way of teaching (Barazangi 1990b). Without challenging the discourse of the discipline in both "Islamic" and other schools (Abd-Allah 1998) and at universities (M. al Faruqi 1998), and without challenging present views with regard to woman's emancipation and human rights as well as the Muslim dogmatic approach, there can be no innovation in the manner explained earlier.

As stated in my 2004 essay "Understanding Muslim Women's Self-Identity and Resistance to Feminism and Participatory Action Research," I consider the relationship of feminism to action research to be analogous to that of the brain and mind. In this book, I am extending the same metaphor to the relationship of self-identified "feminism" and Islamic gender revolution: together they create an active process of individual consciousness and social action. I argue further that the analysis of Muslim women's issues within ethnicity, race, and gender, particularly as presented in contemporary academic discourses, is antithetical to this active process. Muslim women scholar-activists view the academic use of gender and other constructs as factors that play a deactivating role in the conscientious process of self-identification with Islam. This deactivation could explain why some Muslim women scholar- activists resist, and at times even reject, the kind of feminism and activism that emphasize universal group solidarity, as discussed by some essays in Afkhami and Vaziri (1996), not paying attention to the different individual worldviews.

By defining Islam as an action-oriented worldview that encompasses cultural and social elements, including religious beliefs, I emphasize this worldview's reliance on the human capacity to reason and its goal as being that of constructive and just behavior, a goal that will bring about *taqwa*, the equilibrium between individual consciousness and social action within the particular worldview (Qur'an, 5:96).

I understand feminism "as a creative theory of human relations aimed at transforming social structures that dismiss individual contributions, particularly those of females, because these contributions are perceived not to fit the 'cultural standards'" (Barazangi 1999b, 2). Despite my attempts to have feminism understood among my Muslim coresearchers, resistance to it happened on many levels, ranging from rejection to skepticism, and the resistance was more pronounced among those who were affiliated with Western higher education institutions. The working definition of action research I use is "a form of research that generates knowledge claims for the express purpose of taking action to promote social change and social analysis [wherein involved members may] control their destinies and improve their capacities to do so" (Greenwood and Levin 1998, 6). Similarly, but with less skepticism, my Muslim coresearchers were not willing to take social change with the same assumptions. I was also informed by the research findings that unless Muslim men take similar steps in this direction, only minor changes would take place. Finally, most of my coresearchers defined ethnicity as an individual's belonging to a people of distinctive linguistic, racial, or cultural tradition, and were not aware of the conflict between their primary and secondary identifications until I probed further into the premises of the worldview they claim to be Islamic.

In my focus on the relation between knowledge and identity, I find it necessary to balance the tension between the individual Muslim woman and her hegemonic Muslim community. Furthermore, I seek to bring to the surface underlying assumptions about how the tension in the relationship between academic feminists and some Muslim women scholar-activists might be understood and, once understood, changed. In the process, I have unraveled another set of tensions resulting from some researchers' focus mainly on global "solidarity." These tensions manifest themselves on four levels: value claims, knowledge claims, cultural or historical claims, and praxis or socialization claims that I collectively call "worldview claims" (Barazangi 2004).

My goal has been to develop a self-learning process and to build a curricular design that improves the capacity of Muslim women to engage their destinies more faithfully. Faithfulness here means that the Muslim woman will change her perception of her identification with Islam and of her role in society before she is able to change her life situation in the home and in the learning/teaching/research environment and to support self-realization and *taqwa* in the larger social context. It means, in a sense, to bridge individual consciousness and social action in order to bring about a cognitive and attitudinal change on the individual level and, inextricably linked to such change, a transformation in the social structure. Transforming the social structure may mitigate potential dismissal of the Muslim women's worldview by feminists as lacking scholarly validity.

My pedagogical assumption is that once a woman changes what is in herself, she is able to change the social structure (Qur'an, 13:11).[3] I believe that in our work within American academic parameters we have overlooked the power of the (unquestioned and unexamined) Western approach to academic knowledge, and its generation and dissemination process. Specifically, Western approaches have marginalized the worldview of Muslim women both by dismissing their views as "religious" and by taking Muslim male elites' views at face value. This approach has resulted in temporary solutions, which were subsequently dismantled by a backlash from *muqallidun* Muslim male interpreters.

In the rest of this chapter, I will elaborate on the worldview claims to reset the groundwork for a change in viewing Islam as *Din* rather than mere religion. I present my argument by analyzing a historical event and conclude with some implications for Muslim women who ground their authority in the Qur'an.

Islam as a *Din* (a Worldview)

By defining Islam as an action-oriented worldview that encompasses social, cultural, and political elements, including religious and secular *ijtihad*, I emphasize this worldview's reliance on the human capacity to reason and its goal, the construction of fairness (*qist*) in the decision-making process that brings equilibrium (*taqwa*).[4] I specifically wanted to address the tension between feminist-generated conceptions of liberation vis-à-vis Muslim women's initiated leadership. My focus will be on the relation between identity, knowledge, and social and political constructs. Worldview claims determine the understanding of the relationship between Muslim women and the academic community of feminists and Islamic or area study researchers. These claims also determine the implications of these relationships for research and educational intervention (knowledge production and transformation) that is intended not only to promote social justice for Muslim women but also to effect a perceptual and structural transformation in the system toward a sustainable solution.[5]

Value Claims

Within the Qur'anic meaning of knowledge and pedagogy, *taqwa* is the measure by which a course of study or action is considered "Islamic." To place gender as the unit of analysis for social change would therefore contradict the Qur'anic criterion of distinguishing individuals from one another by *taqwa*. Muslim women who work from within the Qur'anic framework rely on reason as the distinctive characteristic of human beings and as the very means that enables individuals to achieve *taqwa*. Feminists' emphasis on gender as a central concept is viewed by Muslim women as simply replacing patriarchal power with feminist power instead of bringing about *taqwa*, balancing individual and social relations. Similarly, activists' focus on social change only is viewed as tipping the balance toward social solidarity without securing individual cognitive and attitudinal transformation that will eventually change the predominant male and Western discourse as well as the complementarities structure. Although I recognize racial, ethnic, gender, and religious differences, and the real material consequences of these differences, in my understanding of the active process of individual consciousness and social action, I do not wish to invoke these differences as the criterion by which to measure social justice and individual self-identification. By theorizing about my consciousness process and that of my coresearchers, I also try to understand and change the politics of knowledge as it relates to Muslim women in general and to my collaboration with some Muslim women in particular. Finally, by acting together with my coresearchers on generating new meanings of the "religious" texts, particularly the Qur'an, we are also presenting new possibilities for the Muslim majority societies to increase their capacity for gender justice.

Knowledge Claims

The goal in the Qur'an is to change the nature of the relationship of the knower (the human) with the natural law from that of domination into that of balanced creativity. "Do they not travel through the land, so that their hearts (*qulub*) [and minds, or conscience] may comprehend wisdom, and their ears may thus learn to hear? Truly it is not their eyes that are blind, but their hearts that are in their breasts" (Qur'an, 22:46). To realize the subtle and less subtle epistemological relationship between Muslim women and feminism in higher education institutions, we need to understand the Western academic discourse that created, defined, and attempted to address issues related to Muslim women long before feminism. First, Western academe created a rift not only between seeking knowledge for its own sake and its utilitarian results, but also between the moral and the cognitive processes of scientific inquiry. Second, it is a well-known fact— supported by a substantial body of theoretical arguments and empirical evidence—that a number of Orientalist images and perceptions of the Muslim people and their culture as inferior served the imperial colonial governments and missionaries, dominating views and policies in Muslim/ Arab societies (Said 1978, 1981; M. al Faruqi 1998). What is less known is the fact that the discipline of Middle Eastern studies (MES) not only formed a large research thrust but also resulted in the field of Middle East Women's Studies (MEWS) *without producing sustainable benefits to the women of the region at large.* Muslim women either rejected MEWS or attempted to set their own research agenda, but they found that they could not go far enough in addressing the issues within their own framework, not even the agenda of international development, because it was framed by the Western worldview. Kramer (2001, 6), for instance, argues that MES research is irrelevant to American policy in the region, because MES research does not succumb to American government policies. I argue, instead, that most of this research is indeed irrelevant, *but particularly irrelevant to the people of the region.* MES is a uniquely American area studies discipline. It was created during the cold war. Within the fold of the discipline lies the study of Islam and Muslim societies. Muslim women studies is the youngest field within the discipline, operating inside, as it were, the premises of Orientalism and MES (in addition to those of conventional social and psychological theories, postmodernism, literal critical theory, and feminism). Despite their rich literary production, very few of these studies have made an impact on the lives of the people there, and rarely do they recognize the presence of Muslim women's scholarship in America. The UNDP 2002 report on Arab human development take an honest look at the results and conclude that despite significant strides in more than one area of human development in the last three decades, Arab countries still suffer from three deficits, deficits relating to freedom, empowerment of women, and knowledge (UNDP/HDR 2002: foreword).[6] Moreover, discussions on democratizing Muslim societies hardly acknowledge women's role beyond domestic democracy (Barazangi 2003). Finally, the sequel 2003 Arab Human Development Report (UNDP/HDR 2003) "makes it clear that, in the Arab civilization, the pursuit of knowledge is prompted by religion, culture, history and the human will to achieve success. Obstructions to this quest are the defective structures created by human beings— social, economic and above all political. Arabs must remove or reform these structures in order to take the place they deserve in the world of knowledge at the beginning of the knowledge millennium." One could replace the quantifying identity "Arab" with "Muslim" and the same assertions and findings apply.

Individual consciousness and social epistemological relationship were not balanced among American Muslim women because of the tension between their premises and the premises of Western academic feminists. Although the premises seemed compatible, given that they both were forging an argument for gender justice, Muslim women's relationship with Western academic feminism and academia have remained unchanged (Barazangi 2001). Despite being in the same "critical plane," as Sandra Harding (1987, 11) puts it, the sharing in the production of academic knowledge among Muslim women scholars and Western academic feminists did not actually have a significant impact on the Muslim women scholars' life experiences or on academic policies concerning the understanding of Islam and the Muslim community. The "new knowledge" has not changed the attitude of many feminists. Many still view their Muslim colleagues as the "other," as "women of color," or "third-world women" instead of treating them as agents of change for their own situation, as partners in the struggle for social justice, and as persons whose very lives embody a living experience to learn from. In addition, Muslim women's scholarly work tends to be viewed as some sort of applied sociology or activism. When I argued in 1992 that a course on Muslim women at

Cornell University ought to be taught from the perspective of these women, some of my colleagues accused me of attempting to proselytize Islam.

Historical or Cultural Claims

Academic studies on Muslim women produced many images of these women, but instead of leading to change in their lives, it has actually reinforced the status quo, adding to the prevalent negative images of the "marginal" Muslim woman.[7] In addition to the old philosophy of dichotomized and dichotomizing fields of studies, Western attitudes that emphasize individual liberty have dominated Western academic cultural and historical claims about Muslim societies and "their" women, not realizing that human dignity takes precedence over liberty in Arab/Islamic culture. The divide between humanities and social sciences furthered this dominant dichotomy in understanding Muslim women, thus creating another gap between grassroots and academic feminisms. The studies of Muslim women have been placed either under the heading of humanities (Oriental studies) or the social sciences (area studies of the Middle East, South Asia, and Southeast Asia). Thus, issues of Muslim women are only marginally theorized within feminist and women's studies discourses if at all. How then is it possible to address Muslim women's issues from the moral-cognitive rationality of the Qur'an in this context?

The knowledge structure about Muslim women naturally followed the premises and the cultures of either of the two strands of knowledge in the humanities and in social sciences respectively. Oriental studies rested on the philological decipherment and translation of texts; recently the latter also has become prevalent in literary criticism. Meanwhile, in Middle East studies strategy is viewed as having a role that is more important than either the culture or religion of those studied, let alone their role as subjects instead of objects. W. C. Smith (1956, 108) expounded on the "invalidity" of the disciplines whose approach is marred by a "preoccupation with the techniques and methods rather than with the object of the study, and, correspondingly, with manipulation and control rather than appreciation." As a result, the worldview claims of these women seem to have been lost both at the level of the institution of higher education and within their particular community. The preoccupation of academics with the promotion of "scientific" theories and interpretations of Islam, of Muslims, and of Muslim women has blinded many of them from realizing that in the process they assumed for themselves the role and authority to act as spokespersons for these women and their culture. Meanwhile, Muslim communities have grown either defensive about these theories or suspicious of academicians because the latter were perceived to fulfill the strategy of the colonizing/controlling governments. As a consequence there is a backlash of Muslim authoritarian elites (males and females) on Muslim women who use Western methodologies, arguing that they aid the conspiracy against the Muslim social fabrics.

Socialization Claims

Academic feminism has grown largely oblivious to the scholarship of "others" despite the fact that both its members and academic Muslim women trace their origin to their own suffragist movements. Most of the rich literature resulting from feminist attempts to understand women and gender was produced within the existing discourse of the dichotomous disciplines; hence, the focus on the "self" or the "other" as the problem did not change, either. Furthermore, the pedagogy became so abstract that women's studies began to lose touch with the real issues that face feminist teachers and learners. As I continue to modify and change my own course of action (praxis) to approximate the Islamic goal of *taqwa*, I have hoped to facilitate the same process for my coresearchers and my academic colleagues. By being a member of an institution of higher education, I may have contributed ideas and case studies to feminist theories and ethnographies, through my action research collaboration with some academic Muslim women, but the question remains how such contributions can effectively change academic worldview claims that have uncritically assimilated both feminism and the study of Muslim women.

Social research that does not contribute to and allow for self-determination by involved subjects cannot be validated because it overlooks the inquisitive process that a learner goes through as she or he attempts to make sense of and to act on the nature of knowledge, its origin, and its evolution with the goal of self-realization as a citizen. Furthermore, higher education institutions claim to build a relationship with the surrounding community; however, they have not created enough change in their own structure and policy to be credited with evidence of understanding and caring for the community's input. For a higher education institution to function as a source for understanding communities, then, it needs to understand the community well enough to critically reflect on and make a significant change in its structure and discourse in order to aid the community to change itself. American Muslim women live among a loosely structured community of feminist researchers, like myself, who are part of academia and who claim to understand Muslim women, but whose praxis has hardly begun to be realized. How then could the academic community recognize these women's self-identity with the Qur'an and with Islam as a world-view?

When I speak of self-identity, I am concerned with the Muslim woman's exercise of ability and engagement of the complexities of her life reality in identifying with Islam as an autonomous individual, and in real-izing that without this ability and without reading, interpreting, and ap-plying Islam's guidelines as presented in the Qur'an on her own, she may not be able to claim such an identification. This primary identification will no doubt be affected by the secondary, multiple, socially constructed iden-tities (gender, ethnicity, race, and class) that will factor in her reinterpreta-tion of the text. Thus, the more difficult task for the Muslim woman is that she remain conscious of these factors in every process of her own lit-eracy—be it in her engagement of the text or the world—as well as in her self-identification with Islam. She can and needs to remain conscious of these factors without making them central concepts in analyzing her own problems and in determining her own course of action toward the solution to these problems. But because of the conformity of higher education insti-tutions to a dichotomous knowledge production process (one that sepa-rates out cognitive and moral development and dichotomizes disciplines), such autonomous integration has not been possible. As suggested else-where (Barazangi 1998c), although this integration was achieved through self-learning, some academic Muslim women have not used a metacog-nitive process that integrates the declarative and procedural knowledge process in order to integrate the rational and the moral because they have confused this process with other processes followed either by academe or their community. Muslim women's resistance to the dichotomous aca-demic process has led them to resist Western feminism, rather than to re-sist concepts generated within the academic worldview claims. Muslim women could benefit from feminist-informed action research by learning a number of consciousness-raising strategies and tools for deconstructing hierarchies, for instance. Meanwhile, their resistance to moral hegemony has led them to resist processes of generating knowledge that come from higher education institutions instead of refuting only the interpretations resulting from such processes.

The challenging task for Muslim women, therefore, is to ground and balance their individual autonomy in the context of the social hegemony of academic life, when they themselves and academicians are still operating from within their own different worldview claims. As long as Muslim males perceive themselves as the moral guardians of women and the authority on interpreting the Qur'an, the challenge for Muslim women lies also in balancing their individual autonomy with the heteronomy of the community.

Resolving or Balancing the Tensions

I concluded the earlier section by asking whether it is possible to balance the tension between the different views of Islam, education, and women, particularly the Muslim woman. In this section I will discuss whether it is necessary to resolve this tension and whether resolving it would mean balancing it. Given that the Islamic view of human existence is that humankind is being tested as to whether or not an individual is capable of balancing the tension between the ideals and practice and between individual consciousness and social action, I question whether resolving the tension would lead to balance—*taqwa*—but would be instead against the ontological order of humanity as the Qur'an states. Although I have argued for higher Islamic learning for Muslim women as key to the solution for the dichotomous educational systems in the societies and communities with a majority Muslim population, my intention is not to eliminate or undo this tension since then the human will that is key to human morality becomes unnecessary. In other words, if the duality (or the "two-ness," *izdewajiyah*) in the physical world ensures a balanced order (for example, the balance between day and night, and the balance between biological reproductive complementarities of male and female), it is so because there is no choice in the matter. *What makes a human being different from other physical orders in the cosmos is moral choice and the ability to consciously balance one's behavior. Taqwa* is not simply an ideal but is also a goal and orientation in life practice.

The primary prerequisite to Muslim women's identification with Islam —as a moral-existential choice—is the participation in the reading and interpretation of the text of the Qur'an (Barazangi 2000). Three other prerequisites are needed in order to fulfill the Islamic concept of justice and the human rights declaration, as for example, represented in the Beijing platform for action. First, Muslim women's identification with Islam must be acknowledged by both Muslims and non-Muslims before one can expect women in general to be agents of change instead of receivers of change. Second, Muslim women must formulate their own choice before one can claim that a free identification with Islam is actualized (Barazangi 1997, 44). Third, Muslim women must actualize the pedagogical dynamics of Islam. That is, Muslim women's involvement (or lack thereof) in formulating policies within Muslim communities and societies will be the measuring stick of the pedagogical dynamics of the Qur'an.

One might object by asking how one could contradict or disregard the thousands of volumes of historical documents—from those of Qur'anic *tafasir* to the books of Hadith and ending with the books of *sira* (biographies of the prophet Muhammad). My response to this objection is simple: It is not a question of contradicting or disregarding earlier interpretations nor of rejecting heritage, but a matter of applying the Qur'anic mandate of *"indhuru fi al-ardh,"* "We have made you trustees on earth after them to see how you may act" (Qur'an, 10:14), and "the affair [of the time] belongs to you, [addressing Queen Sheba] so you decide what you want to do" (Qur'an, 27:33). How could I (or anyone else), therefore, be expected to use these "readers" in Islamic history (from Ibn Sa'd's *Tabaqat* to the present World Wide Web pages) for claiming self-identity and for educating oneself and the young generation of Muslim women and men without first acting on what the Qur'anic text guides one to do? Despite their faith in Islam and in the Prophet, and despite their "great" historical achievements in their respective times, Muslims of different ages and regions were not able to modify the prior, that is, traditioned conception of woman's proxy morality, nor of her role as being complementary or secondary to the male.

This is the very reason why contemporary Muslims and some Orientalists alike are still perplexed as to what went wrong in Islamic history. Many scholars often find that shortly after the death of the Prophet, Islam was not fully applied. One can activate the polemic argument that the teachings of Islam were not followed, but the core of the matter is that, to a large extent, Muslims did not apply the Qur'anic pedagogical dynamics to social structures and human relations. They were more concerned with philosophical and individual piety and with political gain, while overlooking the male-female relation as a prerequisite to changing the social structure. Because we do not have enough documentation of the social history of the time—most of the *sira* books emphasize the *maghazi* (conflicts and wars between Muslims and their neighboring tribes and dynasties)—there is no other explanation accessible. Even if we accept the argument of Rubin (1995) that *sira* books were not confined to *maghazi* but indicate the Prophet's extrapolation and practice of the Qur'anic teachings, they cannot replace Qur'anic mandates because those *sira* narratives were external to the Qur'an.

Despite all the "reforms" that we now read about in history and anthropology, we still find that everything is "modernized" in postcolonial Muslim societies except the personal laws that affect familial and social relations, ranging from marriage to inheritance. If one accepts the argument of Muslim apologists that to keep these personal laws intact is what holds the stability of the family and the structure of Muslim societies together, then one has to apply the Qur'anic criterion of *taqwa* to assess whether such stability is beneficial or harmful to the individual and the society in the long run. How could one change a society without changing individual conceptual and attitudinal structures? Does the Qur'an not remind human beings that "God may not change *what with* a people until they change *what is in* themselves" (13:11)? One could also activate the argument of political scientists that because *khilafah* was moved into the sphere of mere political leadership, which was made hereditary to male lineage (see, for example, what the Shi'ah propagate, or what Mua'wiyah, the first Ummayad caliph, has done), but these are only symptoms, symptoms resulting from a lack of change in kinship and sexuality conceptions, particularly concerning one-half of the Muslim community, namely the female population. In addition, by being responsible for bringing up the next generations of Muslims, the voice of this half of the population was lost perpetually. Thus, misconceptions flourished and were reinforced again and again and much earlier than Muslim analysts have been willing to admit to—this is more an internal problem than an external one. The misconception and misapplication of Isma'il al Faruqi's (1982a) *Islamization of Knowledge* into a politicized Islam, for example, has generated more conflict in these societies and between them and other societies.

To illustrate the above argument further, I would now like to offer the reader the kind of analysis that is needed, the reflexive pedagogical reading of the Qur'an for which I have argued in this book. When I read about the Prophet's attempt to divorce his second wife, Sawda Bint Zum'ah, and about how she "gave up" her allocated day and night to the third wife, 'A'isha, in order to remain his wife (*Tabaqat Ibn Sa'd* 1904–40, 8:35), I wonder about the pedagogical implications of stories written 150 years after the death of the Prophet. That is, I have to understand the prophetic extrapolation of Qur'anic mandates concerning divorce and being just, especially to wives (the practices of polygyny and exchanging wives were known prior to Islam) ('Abd al-'Ati 1977, 98), and the Prophet's practice within his own household as an example for his followers. The two available explanations are that his practice was conducive to the patriarchal social custom of the time (read: entrenched kinship and sexuality factors) as Wadud-Muhsin (1992) and Arkoun (1994, 60) suggest, or that the Prophet was exercising his power to ensure certain political needs of the new community, and therefore withheld the application of Qur'anic mandates for social justice temporarily. Such has been the explanation of Muslim apologists regarding patriarchal interpretations. Given that the directives of the Qur'an and the first purpose of the message of Islam are to do justice, especially to women and to the disfranchised (Rahman 1996), neither explanation is satisfactory. How could the messenger of *"There is no god but God"* call first and foremost for justice and then succumb to social pressure? And how would the individual woman (and man) who believes in such a message understand and explain it within the framework of Islamic justice without contradicting the Qur'anic expectation (9:24) that all individuals follow the divine law over and above the will of others, even when those others are the spouses or parents? How would such a believer accept the social customs as more compelling than the message that is intended to change attitudes about human relations in order to change these customs?

As a matter of fact, the same narrative in Ibn Sa'd's *Tabaqat* discusses Sawda's averted divorce from the Prophet, and attributes the context of the revelation of verse 4:128 to Sawda's appeal to the Prophet not to divorce her, but to keep her under his household and to "let her die as his wife." If we are to accept Ibn Sa'd's narrative, according to which Sawda's appeal is the occasion for the revelation of 4:128: "If a woman has a reason to fear *nushuz* (rebellion, aversion, or disloyalty) in her husband, or *i'radh* (that he might turn away from her), there is no fault in them if the couple settles things between them"—then we also have to accept that there is a contradiction in Ibn Sa'd's narrative.

It is perplexing how Muslims, generation after generation, have used such a narrative without questioning it to emphasize the sacrifice that Sawda has made of herself in order to remain the Prophet's wife, and to idealize such a sacrifice all the while forgetting the intention of the verse in the first place, namely that the fear of the husband's *nushuz* or *i'radh* are legal grounds for a woman to seek divorce. Therefore, the pedagogical implication of such a narrative is that Sawda not only had given up her legal rights but she also did not internalize the meaning of the verse. That is, she not only sacrificed herself, but also the application of the principle intended by the Qur'anic revelation in order to change existing social custom. Furthermore, not only is the internal coherence of the verse and its coherence with the other related verses (such as the second part of verse 4:34 that instructs men what to do when they fear *nushuz* in their wives) compromised; the pedagogical implications of these verses as well as the significance of the role of the Prophet's wives in interpreting and applying these verses is also diminished, if not obliterated!

Now then, if I am to use this historical narrative as evidence of woman's significance as educator (or lack thereof) in Islamic policy making (from revelation to current interpretations), I need to understand the purpose of the Prophet's behavior because any pedagogical interpretation of events requires knowledge of the goals. 'A'isha 'Abd al-Rahman (1968a, 1:7) states that a literary interpretation of the Qur'an needs a masterful knowledge of the language, meaning the Arabic language. I would add that a pedagogical interpretation of the Qur'an needs both knowledge of the language and understanding of the intent. Given that the first verse of chapter 4 of the Qur'an, "Al-Nisa'" (The Women), starts with the exhortation to be in equilibrium with God who created human beings of a single entity, and given that this exhortation is followed in the next verses (4:3–4) by an affirmation of the rights of orphans, stating that if one fears ill treatment of the widows and orphans, one is permitted to marry from among them up to four, under the condition of being equitable and just, it is clear that the tone and the goal of the entire chapter is first and foremost *justice*. Furthermore, given the reminder that a human may never be able to do justice among the many wives (4:3), it is possible that the Prophet's intention in marrying Sawda was merely to take care of her as the widow of a newly converted Muslim man, Sakran ibn 'Amr. Therefore, even with this intention, he might have realized that he could not do *justice* to her (that is, love her as much as he loved 'A'isha), and thus wanted to divorce her. Yet, if I understand the Prophet's intention of taking Sawda as his second wife for reasons of psychological consolation—after the death of his first wife, Khadija, and after Sawda became a widow—I find it all the more difficult to accept the explanation that his reason for divorcing her, as reported by many books, was that Sawda was growing old and no longer appealing to him. Such a narrative, attributed by some to the Prophet's third and most beloved wife, 'A'isha, is particularly perplexing on many levels.

First, the verse concerning divorce clearly states: "Do not expel them [women] from their houses, nor let them go forth, except when they commit a flagrant indecency" (65:1). Therefore, if I am to take Ibn Sa'd's narrative as accurate, I have to assume that the Prophet was going to commit an injustice toward one of his wives, but that injustice was averted by another revelation (4:128). This is the pedagogical significance of the verse that should be emphasized instead. Even the Prophet was reminded of justice as the primary principle by a divine intervention. It is true that the divorce chapter (65) may be a revelation posterior to the incident concerning Sawda—being number 101 in the chronological order of revelation, compared to number 100 for the women's chapter (chapter 4), according to the *Concordance* of Kassis (1983). But if I am to understand Islam in its totality and interpret its different injunctions from within its overall perspective as the *Din al-'adl*, "the religion or the worldview of justice" (Rahman 1996), while affirming human moral choice (Barazangi 2000, 1997; Afzal-ur-Rahman 1982/81), then, as an educator, I need to look for the missing element(s) that, historically speaking, would have led a wife of the Prophet, Sawda—who had accepted Islam voluntarily before she married him and was herself never suspected of *nushuz*—to accept such a behavior from the Prophet of Islam. Given that "the order of the Qur'an was established by the Prophet on divine inspiration according to aesthetic rules and not thematic or chronological rules" (M. al Faruqi 2000, 89), I have to assume that Ibn Sa'd's story was based on a collection of narratives that were compiled later without paying attention to the Qur'anic context of verse 4:128 nor to its relation to 65:1.

Second, I also have to assume that 'A'isha, the third wife of the Prophet, on whose authority a considerable number of his traditions are narrated, did not apply the Qur'anic pedagogy. More precisely, she did not change her prior conception of women being in competition to gain the favor of the males in their household to that of Islamic sisterhood. How is it possible to accept 'A'isha's narrative as reported, indicating her "happiness with Sawda's giving-up the justly allocated day and night to her, because she ('A'isha) was the most beloved wife of Muhammad"? Are we to accept these matters of jealousy between cowives as having a greater priority for the "ideal" women in Muslim history than the Qur'anic teaching of justice? These elements could be missing either from the narrative or from the reality in the lives of Sawda and all of the Prophet's female household, including 'A'isha and his daughter, Fatima, who later would become the wife of 'Ali, his cousin and the fourth caliph.

Third, not only did these early believing women accept Islam voluntarily; all of them are assumed to have been living Islam at its prime within the first established Muslim community. That is, it is assumed that they practiced the principles of Islam in their daily life and worked toward changing the unjust conditions they encountered under different laws or social customs. In summary, these women were and are understood to be—often in idealized images—the first agents of change in the social structure of their time and the very persons who would effect a change in history, beginning in and with the first Muslim community. But, when one reads Ibn Sa'd's narrative, one must ask whether they really were agents of change.

My consciousness of the Qur'an suggests that Sawda, and perhaps other wives of the Prophet along with other early Muslim women, may not actually have applied the full pedagogy of Islam in the Qur'anic sense that God may not change what with a people until they change what is in themselves (13:11) that should have caused a change in the existing conceptions and attitudes concerning themselves. This would mean that Sawda and others were either not given the tools to understand Islamic injunctions outside the accepted social norms and customary practices (a possibility that is still strongly evidenced among contemporary Muslims), or they did not have enough influence to fully reject the customs and norms that contradicted Qur'anic views. Either reason may have been the consequence of not being fully involved in the decision-making process of the early Muslim community. Perhaps they were brushed aside at the time when such decisions were being made. It is also possible that despite their self-identification with Islam, these women were not prepared to change their own attitude about women's role (that is, they did not change their prior concepts about women's leadership initiative) and were therefore either not able to theorize (be Qur'nically grounded) or they did not actually practice the Islamic pedagogy to its fullest.

In other words, if we accept that the prophet Muhammad had arrived at the decision of parting with Sawda on his own, and if, according to the narrative, he had sent a message to her to prepare her departure from his household, then his decision *en solos* apparently contradicted the principle of mutual consultation (Qur'an, 42:38). Verse 4:128, cited above, was revealed in favor of women, asking the Prophet to reverse his decision and to retain Sawda. This shows that in this incident the Prophet was acting as a man whose actions should be understood within the social constraints of the time (Wadud-Muhsin 1992). The context of 4:128 also offers evidence that there were some elements missing, missing either in the reporting about the Prophet's pedagogical application of the Qur'an or missing in his actual application within his own personal affairs. But on what grounds could or should we not create such a division between Muhammad as a prophet and Muhammad as a man? Is there room in the Qur'anic view to allow for the separation of private and public affairs? The fact that Sawda according to the narrative had to negotiate with him because he was a prophet, to remain part of his household while giving up her natural rights as a wife, affirms again that some elements are missing in the narrative. I may accept the argument that Sawda was a pious woman and "did not care for men," as the narrative states; I may accept that it was more important for her to die as a prophet's wife; but all this does not justify her behavior when such an argument is counter to the discourse of human morality in Islam. According to Islamic morality, a woman need not give up her basic natural rights for the sake of being the Prophet's wife if her husband does not treat her justly, even if he is a prophet (see Qur'anic stories of Zulikha, the wife of the pharaoh, and others). Nor is a human, Islamically speaking, considered autonomously moral if she accepts a worldview that sacrifices justice for the sake of being someone's wife, even the Prophet's.

The Qur'anic message is intended for this: to change the social structure and eventually to eliminate oppressive practices, to reverse prior conceptions of woman's morality, and eventually to restore human dignity. Hence, such narratives need to be reanalyzed conceptually and deconstructed within the Qur'anic framework before they can be used as evidence that speaks to the role these women played in early Islamic history.

Unfortunately the narrative in Ibn Sa'd, and many like it, was taken to represent, incontrovertibly, the "ideal pious Muslim woman" who remains obedient to her husband because he is the Prophet (the Prophet's orders may not be disobeyed), and was also generalized to apply to all women who thus could not disobey their husbands since they would be considered rebellious, as the second part of verse 4:34, in the same chapter, has been interpreted. Not only has this interpretation of the second part of the verse been confused in its context with that of the first part, in which, contrary to the Qur'anic teaching of men's economic responsibility toward their female household, men claim to have the upper hand over women (see chapter 4; and M. al Faruqi 2000, 86–89). It reinforces many misunderstandings of the message of Islam and has thus resulted in injustice, injustice not only to women but also to the Qur'an. How is it possible to teach the first prerequisite of Islamic morality, the freedom to choose or not to choose Islam as a worldview that affirms God as the source of knowledge and value (Barazangi 2000, 1997; Afzal-ur-Rahman 1982, 2:10), when we demand of young girls and women to live in blind obedience to another human being, even when that human happens to be her husband, and to do so when her basic rights are being violated? Similar injustices to the Qur'an occur when 4:1–3 is interpreted in favor of men, giving them license to marry more than one woman and forgetting the two conditions of living justly, namely, that a human is incapable of being just in his affection to more than one wife at a time and that, as shown above, the context speaks to multiple marriages only in the case of widows and orphans.

Epilogue

To self-identify with Islam's goal of justice is to actualize a sound philosophical and theoretical grounding, to enter the pedagogical dynamics for building gender justice in Muslim societies and communities, and thus to engage the action-oriented Islamic worldview. The goal of bridging feminist views or any other and the Islamic worldview is gender justice and to create a transformative approach to the generation of knowledge that includes women and men on the level of conception and of practice.

For Muslim women to achieve this goal, they need direct access to, and conscientious knowledge of the Qur'an, and they need to be able to engage in autonomous action that is void of intermediaries, whether the institutionalized views of academe or the views of the community. Instead, feminism has focused more on the generation of knowledge than on the persons whose issues and indigenous knowledge became, in that process, obscured behind the curriculum. A learner who consciously chooses the feminist worldview as her primary reference actually furthers a broad sense of feminism; however, unless she reclaims education unto and for herself (looking beyond feminist theories and the curricula), she cannot self-identify with her worldview goals. That is, she not only needs to free herself from all that which—within and outside her own self—would demand obedience to whatever social construction of gender. She effectively needs to free the curriculum from the hidden discourse(s) by exposing the existing ideological and scholarly dichotomies between the two views of Western and traditional Muslim interpretations of Islam. These dichotomies exist in both the content and the form of the curriculum and in the underlying premises, just as they exist between the ideals and practice of the traditional liberal arts curriculum and the Muslim community. Since the former emphasizes "objectivity" without appreciating the variations in worldviews and the latter a "subjective" belief system without allowing individual autonomous rationality and morality, the dichotomies extend further by influencing the dichotomies between the disciplines (of both Islamic studies and Muslim women's studies) in the curriculum.

Not being able to free themselves from the constraints of a biologically focused gender identification and from the juxtaposition of the social sciences versus the humanities, academic feminists have gradually become less connected with grassroots activism and more removed from everyday issues, while becoming increasingly "respectable" within academia. The more abstract the discipline of women's studies has become, the less autonomous it has grown, as have the majority of its members. It should surprise no one, therefore, when I argue that feminism has helped us to understand better the notion of the hidden curriculum but did not help itself in being understood and practiced.

To move away from conventional scholarly views, including that of academic feminism, and into the view of human moral and cognitive autonomy may shed new light on understanding Muslim woman and her education from within her own view of Islam and its premises in a manner similar to the interactive rationality of Benhabib (1992). For such rationality not to exclude individual human experience, however, we need to create space for individuals' ability to understand their own particularity in order to become universal and interactive (Barazangi 1993). The action-oriented Qur'anic worldview may help an individual to ground her (or his) understanding of Islam, while action research might move this experience from the particular into the universal without imposing one's voice or view. However, unless each individual remains vigilant of her (or his) individual consciousness and its worldview claims, her worldview will be uncritically assimilated by the institutional views just as was the case with the medieval church and with most academic feminism.

Perhaps non-Muslims, particularly those interested in Muslim women's development, by becoming more aware of Muslim women's worldview and not only looking at Muslim women through the issues of the veil, politics of difference, or globalization, could responsibly participate in and benefit themselves from balancing the action-oriented research. Similarly, Muslim women feminists may benefit themselves and others by unveiling their conscious process in order to make their worldview claims accessible. The third possibility of a balanced action-oriented research becomes available when academic institutions not only claim to affirm reason as the distinct characteristic of their operation, but to recognize that for the learner conscientious choice goes hand-in-hand with reason if effective learning is to be achieved. Free conscious choice affirms reason being also essential for personal identity, and in order to "move beyond the metaphysical assumptions of the Enlightenment universalism" (Benhabib 1992, 5–6). Therefore, in order for the process of *taqwa* to move toward completion, we need first to replace these assumptions because they have ignored the individual worldview, and, hence, have separated reason from moral and ethical premises; second, replace the human domination of nature with a creative understanding of natural law and of the divine guidance; third, replace human domination over other humans by dedicating ourselves to the practicing of *taqwa*, specifically in how we discuss, examine, and engage the different worldviews—be they Islamic or non-Islamic.

Notes

Introduction: Woman's Identity and the Qur'an

1. AH (*anno Hegirae*) marks the years following the prophet Muhammad's migration (*hijra*) from Mecca to Medina and his establishment of the first Muslim community in circa AD 623.

2. Note that Islamic higher learning has been both my goal and the methodology by which I approach my work on Islamic education. Just as I recommend it for other women to gain their identification with Islam, I have pursued my self-learning and self-teaching with the Qur'anic worldview and am now complementing this work with a pedagogical reading of the Qur'an.

3. I disagree with Arkoun's separation of religion from reason (1994, 2). The Qur'an states: "We have brought to you the reminding message (*al-dhikr*), so you may extrapolate for the people what was sent to them, and hence they may think rationally (*yatafakkarun*)" (16:44).

4. A respected colleague sent me an e-mail communication on December 2, 1998, concerning Muslims' work on education, to the effect that although she disagrees with males' policies, she is executing those policies because there is no one else to "get the job done." Throughout this book, I revisit the concept of self-sacrifice always expected of females, especially among religious groups, versus the teaching of self-realization that is enjoined by the Qur'an. The realization of oneself as an intellectually, spiritually, and morally autonomous human being is of paramount importance for leadership initiatives.

5. See Arkoun's analysis of the "image" versus the realistic (1994, 1–3, n1, n4).

6. Arkoun discusses the necessity of joining erudite research with reflective activity because, in his words, it is "an absence of reflection about principles and founding values of the Islamic tradition that has permitted contemporary Islam to veer into mythological and ideological detours" (1994, 3).

7. Note here that although I considered in my early works the argument that Western and Muslim patriarchy were at work against females as suggested, for example, by Mernissi (1991, 1987), my empirical research findings suggest that the problem is beyond patriarchy.

8. See Barazangi (1999b) for further analysis of the imperative to change the structure of the system for the woman to change her worldview and to achieve her self-realization.

9. Note here that Asma Afsaruddin (2003) may have begun this task in her "Obedience to Political Authority: An Evolutionary Concept." Also, see Abou El Fadl, 1997.

10. Azizah al-Hibri seems to have started this task in her "A Study of Islamic Herstory: Or How Did We Ever Get into This Mess?" (1982), but to my knowledge there was no expansion on this topic.

11. Note here that Asma Barlas (2002) discusses both the concepts of vicegerency and morality, and she reads the Qur'anic text holistically, but she also reads it as a historically situated text and distinguishes her work by engaging with feminist critiques using their own terms and concepts.

12. Such views were emphasized even when a Muslim woman was granted the 2003 Nobel Peace Prize. Shirin Ebadi, who has been a "tireless and peaceful activist for democracy and the rule of law as well as a courageous human-rights lawyer in Iran's Islamic Republic," was reported to have said: "We need *an Islam* that is *compatible with democracy* and one that's respectful of individual rights" *(my emphasis)* (*Christian Science Monitor*, October 14, 2003). Although it is an important and positive step toward recognizing a Muslim woman's struggle, to speak of "an Islam that is compatible with" something implies that there is more than one Islam. It also reinforces the view that Islamic values are still being compared with Western-based human rights standards without attempting to understand them on their own terms.

13. See http://www.rawa.org for "Green Demands Invitation of Afghan Women to Bonn Talks on the Future of Afghanistan" (accessed November 27, 2001). The report tells how Afghani women were in fact marginalized and largely excluded from participating in the Afghan peace process while many claims were being made for Afghan women's liberation. Examples of such claims were NOW (the National Organization of Women) speaking on behalf of Afghan women facing the Taliban in 1997, and Laura Bush's declaration that the war in Afghanistan was to "liberate the Afghan women" (http://www.whitehouse.gov/news/releases/2001/11/20011117.html, accessed April 27, 2003).

14. Riffat Hassan (1991) narrates her mother's discontent with her father's traditionalism, as well as her inability to understand why Riffat had to change some of these traditions by leaving home to study abroad. Her narrative could be used to describe the views prevalent among many women in the Muslim world.

15. In her PhD dissertation, Etin Anwar (2002) discusses gender and self in Islam, but the emphasis is on philosophical interpretation. By contrast, my early attempt was to use education as a means to free oneself from *shirk* (that is, the opposite of *Tawhid*, Oneness of the Deity and the source of value and knowledge) (Barazangi 1982). A similar work is Mona Hammam's (1977) PhD dissertation, in which she argues for the practice of freedom as education. Another related work is Zakia Belhachmi's (2000) PhD dissertation, in which she questions the scientific merit of Mernissi's and Sa'dawi's feminist approach to Muslim/Arab culture.

16. Barazangi (1992) reports on the informal participatory survey among the 150 women attending NACMW's founding meeting.

17. Maysam al Faruqi also contributed a paper titled "Self-Identity in the Qur'an and Islamic law" during the MESA 1995 panel and to *Windows of Faith*.

18. A search conducted in August 1998 generated only 14 citations related to education out of the 496 citations related to Muslim women in the Library of Congress database. In December 2002, the number was 14 of 651.

19. See Rahman's distinction between the *Sunnah* of the Prophet and the *sunnah* of the community (prior practices) and his argument for their organic relationship (1995).

20. Denis L. Soufi writes in the abstract of "The Image of Fatima in Classical Muslim Thought" (1997): "For Sunnis, Fatima is often portrayed as an ordinary pious woman, both in her mundane roles as daughter, wife, and mother, but she occasionally rises to the rank of sainthood. For Shiʿa, Fatima's role as the feminine counterpart to the Imams creates a woman who displays the characteristics of the ideal Muslim woman in a way that makes her further out of reach as a role model for Muslim women than the Imams are for Muslim men. In addition, she is often used as a foil to ʿAli, thus undermining her idealization." See further discussion of the idealization of women in chapter 2 of this book.

Chapter 1. Pedagogical Reading of the Qur'an

1. The first date indicates the Hijra year, while the second indicates the AD (anno Domini) year.

2. Amina Wadud-Muhsin published a 1999 edition of her 1992 book under the name Amina Wadud.

3. I wrote the following communiqué questioning a proposed change in the ISNA and MSA constitutions, addressing my June 17, 2001, e-mail to ISNA president Dr. Siddiqui and several Muslim organizations:

This message is intended for all Islamic/Muslim organizations of North America and their members.

On February 8, 2001, ISNA Election Committee sent a letter to its members calling for nomination of new officers, also asking to vote on a revision in the ISNA Constitution. An extremely disturbing phrase was included under Article VIII.1.1.b. The phrase reads as follows: "Five members to be elected by the general body of ISNA membership, with provision for special representation, such as sister members electing sisters."

On June 8, 2001, the Association of Muslim Social Scientists (AMSS) Election Committee also sent a letter to its members calling them to vote to a slate of candidates, stating: "Select the number of candidates for each position as indicated. You may also write in other candidates, including Muslim sisters for whom you may want to vote."

It seems that these male-run committees either lack the imagination or the courage to find a name of a Muslim woman scholar-activist who is qualified to serve. I am still dreaming of a day when these male Muslim establishments wake up to realize how degrading is this trend to all Muslims, especially women, and to recognize the importance of women's role and contribution to Islamic/Muslim decision-making process. This kind of constitutional revisions or ballots require apologies.

4. Erfan Viker, media and communication officer of the American Muslim Council (AMC) wrote a commentary on the role of women in an e-mail message to AMC members on October 14, 2002. Although he was sincere in bringing the voice of the Muslim woman into the fold of such organizations, the mere thought of women's participation as an add-on or an afterthought is the core of the problem that I am addressing.

5. Jawdat Sa'id had several works as part of this reading. Primary among them is *Madhhab Ibn Adam al-Awwal, aw Mushkilat al-'Unf fi al-'Amal al-Islami* (first published in 1966, and a third printing was in 1984), in which he affirms Islam's peaceful resistance and distinguishes between jihad (struggle of a leader) after being elected by the people in order to ensure justice, and fighting to gain political power.

6. It is obvious that I am limited by my knowledge of Arabic and English. Readings of the Qur'an in other Islamic or non-Islamic languages may be equally important.

7. Frederick Denny (1989, 99), quoting Rahman.

8. Rahman (1995, 1) explains the confusion between the *Sunnah* denoting actual behavioral practice of the Prophet and *sunnah* as an element of moral ought, an established normative standard of the community.

Chapter 2. The Religio-Moral-Rational Characteristics of the Qur'an and the Story of Creation

1. Note that although my contention may further be supported by Arkoun's argument that the Qur'anic laws of inheritance were not completely interpreted or applied for fear of losing the pre-Islamic paternal rights to property (Arkoun 1993, 52), I steer away from such argument not only because it was based on other studies whose methodology is not corroborated by the Qur'an, but also because it is secondary to the purpose of this book.

2. Barazangi (1997) cites Hind Bint 'Utbah. Malek Bennabi (1968, 338) cites 'A'isha's reaction when her father asked her to thank the Prophet for restoring his trust in her after the revelation of 24:3–4 to vindicate 'A'isha from the accusation of unfaithfulness. 'A'isha was reported to have replied: "By Allah, I will not thank him [Muhammad], I will not thank but Allah."

3. Note that the word *hijab* in Arabic and as used in the Qur'an means a curtain or divide, but it has been misused to indicate the woman's attire (see further details in chapter 3).

4. See the difference between the translation of Genesis 2:21–25 in the New English Bible (1970), and what is stated in an earlier version of Genesis, that Elizabeth Cady Stanton interpreted in 1895 (*The Woman's Bible*, 1972 reprint).

5. See Barazangi (1988, 120) on the distinction between the *Sunnah* of the Prophet and its expansion to include the *sunnah* of the companions of different eras or the traditions of religious scholars.

6. See Rahman (1965) for further explanation of *ijma'* and on the difference between *Sunnah* and *sunnah*.

7. See Arkoun's criticism of this static theology of Islam (1994, 2).

8. The most cited example is the description of Maryam (Mary) in the Qur'an wherein she reacts to her tribe's accusation of lack of chastity by secluding herself behind a *hijab* (curtain) and responding with a fast of silence (Qur'an, 19:16–26).

9. I explain in chapter 3 how Muslims limit the meaning of the ideal Muslim woman when they view Mary's celibacy and seclusion as the ideal for the Muslim woman's modesty and chastity, or when they interpret the meaning of *hijab* in the Qur'an (33:53) as a license to seclude women or segregate them.

10. See Elizabeth Cady Stanton's quote in the introduction concerning self-development as a higher duty than self-sacrifice, and this author's argument that self-development may not be realized without self-identity.

11. Paulo Freire (1970) is known among educators for the phrase "learning the word by reading the world."

12. There are 123 verses in total that speak of Adam, including verse 2:37, in which it is stated, "Adam has received words [of revelation] from God, and God relented toward Adam."

13. See further explanation in my discussion of the effect of Christian missionaries on Islamic pedagogy (Barazangi 1995b). The interpretation of the sacred was transformed into a task that only elite males may perform as the carriers of the trust, wrongly translated as the "burden." This is further evidenced in Christian theology that relies on interpreting the message of *khilafah* as that of the burden that Christ is believed to carry for the salvation of all humans (Kenneth Cragg, oral presentation, "Two Sacred Paths: Christianity and Islam: A Call for Understanding" conference, Washington National Cathedral and National Cathedral School, Washington, D.C., November 6–7, 1998).

14. See further discussion on proxy morality in chapter 3.

15. Wadud's intention was to interpret the Qur'an from a feminist perspective in order to make explicit the Qur'anic positive stance on women. I am not implying that she intended gendered interpretation.

16. See Barazangi, Zaman, and Afzal (1996, 5–6) for further analysis of how making the principles of the Qur'an particular to maleness vis-à-vis femaleness may have caused gender injustice by stripping women of their moral being and, eventually, excluding them from public participation, such as making Friday congregational prayer obligatory only for males.

17. See the response of 'A'isha to her father, Abu Bakr, in note 2 above.

18. See Rubin's analysis of the layers of the texts about Muhammad, the Prophet of Islam, in the commentaries and books of *fiqh* (1995).

Chapter 3. Autonomous Morality and the Principle of Modesty

1. This expression, "to do the task even when not in agreement with the leader's opinion," was used in a personal communication (November 16, 1998) with a colleague, a Muslim scholar, in reference to the condescending attitudes of her Muslim male supervisor.

2. Ingrid Mattison, one of the interviewees in the video (*The Ideal Muslim Husband*, 1997), asserts the complementary role of women.

3. Note here that Rahman (1965, ix) asserts that "the fundamental importance of the four principles, the Qur'an, the *Sunnah, Ijtihad,* and *Ijma'*—which, it must be emphasized, are not only principles of Islamic jurisprudence, but of all Islamic thought—can hardly be overestimated."

4. I differentiate between cognitive integration and assimilation (1988); also, I distinguish between social tolerance, on the one hand, and conceptual and attitudinal change in the educational process, on the other (1998b).

5. I should note that Fadwa El Guindi (1999) has significantly contributed to the clarity of these terms. However, by using anthropological methodology, her analysis of the text of the Qur'an is based on the socioanthropological practice of these concepts and how such practice influences understanding the relationship between the woman's choice of attire and her role in the society. As is explained in the rest of this chapter, it will not be possible to change the view on the status of Muslim women without changing the way the Qur'an is being interpreted or the way these concepts are being perceived and practiced.

6. I have emphasized "their women" (*nisa'ihenn*) because it is another example (in addition to the example of "*zinah*" as discussed in the introduction) of controversy in common interpretations. Some explain "their" to mean the Muslim women, and others interpret it to mean only the women of the categories of men mentioned above. Yet a third interpretation explains it to mean women in general. Shahrur (2000, 366) explains "*nisa'ihenn*" to mean a plural of *nas'*, that is, the later relatives (such as grandson, and grandchildren in general) who were not mentioned individually in the Qur'an. This latter interpretation is more in harmony with my emphasis on the variation in meanings of *zinah*.

7. See www.al-Islam.com/Quran or /hadith.

8. Shahrur (2000, 363) differentiates between obvious *juyub* (the cleavages between and under the bosoms) that are a lesser *'awra*, and hidden ones (the cleavages of the vagina and the buttocks) that are restricted to the husband (the legal sexual partner). Those detailed explanations might be pertinent to the meaning of *haya'*, but they are not pertinent to my emphasis on the implications of modesty for the role of women in determining blood and marriage relations for lineage and inheritance purposes.

9. See El Guindi (1999). Also, Shahrur (2000, 364) explains *khimar* to mean a covering of the mind (something that affects the mind), not only the head. That is, by being used in verse 24:31 in the context of covering the bosoms, it implies the meta-

phoric meaning of covering their minds, or not understanding the relevance of modesty to the bosoms as a measure to prevent abuse of lactation lineage.

Chapter 4. Gender Equality (al-Musawah) and Equilibrium (Taqwa)

1. I am differentiating between Islamic *Shari'a* (with capital *S*) and *shari'a* (with lowercase *s*), which is commonly used interchangeably with "Islamic law." The first refers only to the Qur'anic system (*shar'* or *minhaj*), while the second may include the prophetic extrapolation and interpretations of commentators and jurists, and other human interpretations.

2. See my (1999b) discussion of the difference between learners' needs as perceived by educators and a learner's interests as perceived by the learner herself.

3. My translation from the Arabic text of 'Abd al-Rahman's *Al-Mafhum al-Islami li Tahrir al-Mar'ah* [Islamic Concept of Woman's Emancipation] (1967, 10).

4. 'Abd al-Rahman is the first female scholar, to my knowledge, to produce a literal reading of the Qur'an, *Al-Tafsir al-Bayani lil Qur'an al-Karim* (1968a). Also, she has written more than two hundred books and papers on the subject of the Qur'an, women, and other literary matters (cf. Mohja Kahf 1998).

5. See my essay (1996, 87–88) for further explanation of these contexts and the confusion about these verses.

6. See the details of the Qur'anic injunctions about *wassiyah* (will) and *irth* (inheritance) in Ibrahim Fawzi's *Ahkam al-Irth* (1987, 49–54). See also Shahrur's detailed treatment of the relationship of *wassiya* to *irth* and of the actual meaning of the different shares, refuting the interpretation that a male gets twice as much as a female (2000, 222–29).

7. It is worth noting that a young female Muslim scholar, after writing a whole thesis decomposing the concept of "*hijab*," in which she argued that *hijab* was not required, decided not to publish the thesis for fear of controversy.

8. See my essay (2002) for an explanation of these problems.

9. Brand (1998, 105, n19) describes Toujan al-Faysal's other encounters with the Jordanian Muslim Brotherhood, which led to a fatwa (decree) against her insisting that her marriage be dissolved (as she was no longer a Muslim)!

10. Examples of Muslims' elevating the Sunnah to the level of the Qur'an are found in Ignac Goldziher (1971).

11. Narrated in *Tarikh Ibn Asaker*. See Umar Rida Kahhalah's *A'lam al-Nisa'* (1977, 5:268).

12. As explained in chapter 3, *hijab* (from Arabic) means curtain, or a physical divider. This term was used in the context of ordering the early Muslims to respect the privacy of the prophet Muhammad's wives, and to respect their private dwellings, which surrounded the Prophet's mosque, a public space (Qur'an, 33:53). In the early twentieth century, some Muslim scholars, including Syed Abul'Ala al-Maudoodi (1967) and Hasan al-Banna (1983), extended this meaning to the form of modest clothes for all Muslim women, resulting in two misconceptions: first, referencing the woman's head cover (*khimar*) as "*hijab*," and confusing the word

"jilbab" (Qur'an, 33:59), in reference to women's outer garment or cloak, with *hijab;* and second, extending the use of *hijab* from mere respect for women's privacy and as a primary principal in lineage relations to implying complete segregation between the sexes.

13. Fatima Mernissi emphasizes the veil in her 1991 and 1987 works. Also, both Mernissi (in a panel discussion during the Sisterhood Is Global conference, "Religion, Culture, and Women's Human Rights in the Muslim World," Washington, D.C., 1994) and Nawal Sa'adawi (invited lecture at Cornell University, 2000) expressed this "enslavement" sentiment in the course of chastising the conservative religious elites for their view of Muslim women. Meanwhile, Katherine Bullock (2003) and her reported interviewees view *hijab* as liberating.

Chapter 5. Self-Identity and Self-Learning: A Shift in Curriculum Development

1. See my essay (1991a) for elaboration on the meaning of integrative curriculum. This curricular framework is also the result of a long-range research project sponsored in part by a 1993–95 grant from the International Council for Adult Education for a collaborative project on a transformative women's literacy in the United States and Pakistan; a 1994 visiting fellowship at Oxford University's Centre for Islamic Studies to lecture on and research the history of Muslim women's education; a 1995–97 Fulbright scholarship to Syria to develop a research-based computerized curriculum in the Arabic environment; and 1999 and 2002 United Nations Development Program TOKTEN fellowships, also to Syria, to develop Web-based curricular framework also in the Arabic environment. During these five 3-month visits, I also conducted participatory action research with Muslim/Arab women grassroots groups.

2. Some theories—using principles of Islamic gender justice, Islamic philosophy of knowledge, Islam's learning and internalization in general, and practices in education and in feminist studies—methodologies, and major findings of this research were partially reported in different publications. In this work, I present the totality of the theories, methodologies, and findings in a coherent, integrative curricular and instructional framework, with the goal of changing the policy-making process.

3. See Anderson's definitions of the two types of knowledge as quoted in O'Malley and Chamot (1990, 20–25, 27–28). Also see implications for Islamic education and the distinction between Islamic (the ideal) and Muslim (the practice), with the implications for instruction, in my essay "Religious Education" (1995a).

4. Note here that the reference to *madrasah* is to the tenth-century Nizam al-Mulk's establishment of the first government-sponsored public educational system and curricular development process. See further explanation in Shalabi (1993, 1979, 1966).

5. For further explanation of a research-based curriculum development, see my article "Arabic Language Learning: A Module of a Research-Based Computerized Curriculum" (1998c).

6. The recent recommendation is that a law should be passed banning "conspicuous" religious symbols. That such symbols would include head scarves worn by Muslim girls is not only alarming but also presents striking evidence for my argument. Furthermore, the French Commission on Church-State Relations urged the passage of such a law while recommending "the teaching of the ideal of secularism and 'solemn adoption' of a character of secularism that will be distributed widely" (*San Francisco Chronicle*, December 12, 2003, A2). If such a practice is not counter to the claimed democratic, liberal process, then what might be?

7. For an example, see the degrading remarks of a member of the South Carolina State Board of Education. Dr. Jordan said in the heated argument about placing the plate of the Ten Commandments in schools: "Screw the Buddhists and kill the Muslims" (May 12, 1997, as reported by the Associated Press). His statement indicates exactly the point that I am emphasizing. That is, our pluralism has not become cognitively and morally autonomous. Individuals are still struggling between their normative beliefs and the "rational" presentation of others' beliefs. They have not yet come to a point where they autonomously are able to integrate the two views, or make sense of them within their own frame of reference. Whether the reason is ignorance or pure refusal to accept the other's norms is a matter for educators to assess. But the results are still strikingly suggestive that unless such individuals are able to understand and undertake cognitive egalitarianism on their own, any attempt to have them accept social egalitarianism will continue to be a weak point in the system, and there is apt to be a backlash with a change of circumstances. This argument became more evident in the aftermath backlash on Muslims and Arabs after September 11, 2001. (See, for example, reports of the American-Arab Anti-discrimination Committee, http://www.adc.org.)

8. For example, Pat Robertson likened Muslims to Nazis; Jerry Falwell called the prophet Muhammad a terrorist (CBS Evening News Report, November 18, 2002).

9. In this context, I argue against Barbara Morris's definition of change agent as one who changes people's beliefs without their knowledge (1979, 15). I suggest this kind of person might be called a manipulator, because agency requires full consciousness.

10. See, for example, my essays listed in the bibliography.

11. In a database search conducted in 1998 on religion and education, I found only six references out of 450 related to Islam, and none of them is concerned with American Muslims. There are several publications known to me as an educator, but for some reason, they are not being indexed by mainstream bibliography indexing agencies. The efforts of Susan Douglass at the Council on Islamic Education with regard to world history in textbooks (1995 and 1994) are the most recognized among mainstream educators, but they were not indexed then. It was only after September 11 that they started to appear in some indices.

12. For example, most of the work of Susan Douglass (noted above) appears as a publication of the Council on Islamic Education (CIE), and often the spokesperson is the CIE director instead of Douglass herself.

13. See Fareed Nuʿman's American Muslim Council report (1992); B. Seits's "Islam Bursting on American Scene" (1998); ABC News, http://www.abcnews.com/sections/world/Americanism 1125 (accessed December 1989).

14. My description of Islam's treatment as window dressing is somewhat related to Banks's (1993) description of the contribution approach. My use of the term, however, is intended to show how educators confuse "Islam" and "Islamic" as the ideal when discussing a negative event that is done by a "Muslim." They also use "Islamic" instead of describing the individual by his or her varied ethnic background or features. This confusion is either intended, because American educators do not want to make distinctions between religious and ethnic elements, or merely a result of ignorance of the difference.

15. Although Banks's (1993) framework provides for understanding the macro- and the micro-cultural elements, it is not sufficient for understanding the relationship of ethnicity to religio-moral rationality, and their relationship to the ideals of secular, liberal society vis-à-vis actual practices in the larger society, particularly with reference to women and underprivileged groups.

16. See, for example, Muhammad (1998).

17. See, for example, Khaliijah Mohammad Salleh, "The Role of Men and Women in Society," *Islamic Horizons* 57 (January/February 1997); Syed Ali Ashraf (1985); and Ahmad and Sajjad (1984).

18. See http://www.Soundvision.com/publicschool/pub.involve.html (accessed August 3, 1999).

19. See, for example, Jamila al-Hashimi, "Public School System versus Islamic School," *Islamic Horizons* 55 (June/July 1997), in which she reasons that the public schools' decline is the result of their attempt to make "the school increasingly the carrier of all kinds of social policies" instead of doing its job "to teach children elementary knowledge skills." In the same breath she states: "Religious groups, in general, have a head start on teaching values in school." It is exactly this dichotomy in education that is creating problems in our educational system. See another type of dichotomy in Hare's (1992, 113–30) discussion of Wilson's (1964) distinction between the method and the content of education vis-à-vis indoctrination. In addition, Muslims are also, knowingly or unknowingly, reinforcing the practice of following precedent, contrary to Qurʾanic injunction, as discussed in chapter 2.

20. See Barazangi's "Religious Education" (1995a) for the distinctions between "Islamic education," "Muslim education," and Western, secular education or universal schooling.

Conclusions. Where Do We Go from Here?

1. The preliminary results in Barazangi et al.'s (2004) "Evaluation Model of Undergraduate Action Research Program" indicate that the college students who were involved in the program were innocent of research skills, other than taking notes and going to the library. Furthermore, because most colleges still operate within traditional education models that follow either the Factory Model metaphor or what is

known as the naturalistic or responsive approaches to schooling, college students continue to be passive learners.

2. See the analysis of the BOCES teachers being in the same position and fearing a change in "authority" (Barazangi 1999b).

3. Jawdat Sa'id (1987) devotes an entire book to the discussion and the implications of this verse.

4. The Qur'an states in 3:18 that God is standing firm on justice, meaning that God's qist means that God created a fair world.

5. Although I share Sandra Harding's assessment of "some important tensions between the feminist analysis of such issues and the traditional theories of knowledge and between the feminist epistemologies themselves" (1987, 181), I am here more concerned with the tension between the Islamic worldview that Muslim women accept and whose pedagogy they are keen to practice and the worldview of feminists and participant action researchers.

6. It is worth noting here that despite the fact that the majority population in the Arab countries is Muslim, the reports emphasize their secondary identity as Arabs.

7. One can detect this image easily by understanding Orientalism and the study of Islam. See Maysam al Faruqi, "From Orientalism to Islamic Studies" (1998).

Selected Bibliography

Abbott, Nabia. 1942. *'A'ishah: The Beloved of Mohammed*. Chicago: University of Chicago Press.

'Abd al-'Ati, Hammudah. 1977. *The Family Structure in Islam*. Indianapolis, Ind.: American Trust Publications.

Abd-Allah, Salwa. 1998. "Islamic Curriculum Development in Masjid al-Qur'an Full Time School." *Religion and Education* 25(1):77–86.

'Abd al-Rahman, A'ish. 1987. *Al-I'jaz al-Bayani lil-Qur'an wa Masa'il ibn al-Azraq*. 2nd printing. Cairo: Dar al-Ma'aref.

———. 1968a. *Al-Tafsir al-Bayani lil Qur'an al-Karim*. Cairo: Dar al-Ma'aref.

———. 1968b. *Al-Qur'an wa Huqquq al-Insan*. Khartoum, Sudan: Jami'at Um Durman.

———. 1967. *Al-Mafhum al-Islami li Tahrir al-Mar'ah*. Khartoum, Sudan: Jami'at Um Durman.

Abou El Fadl, Khaled. 1997. *The Authoritative and Authoritarian in Islamic Discourses: A Contemporary Case Study*. 2nd ed. Austin, Tex.: Dar Taiba.

Afkhami, Mahnaz, and Haleh Vaziri, eds. 1996. *Claiming Our Rights: A Manual for Women's Human Rights Education in Muslim Societies*. 3rd ed. Bethesda, Md.: Sisterhood Is Global Institute.

Afsaruddin, Asma. 2003. "Obedience to Political Authority: An Evolutionary Concept." Proceedings of the fourth annual conference of the Center for the Study of Islam and Democracy, Washington, D.C., May 16, 2003. http://www.islam-democracy.org/4th_Annual_Conference-Afsaruddin_paper.asp (accessed November 10, 2003).

Afzal-ur-Rahman. 1987. *Subject Index of the Holy Qur'an*. Delhi: Noor Publishing House.

———.1981/2. *Muhammad, Encyclopedia of Seerah, 2*. London: Muslim Schools Trust.

Ahmad, Anis, and Muslim Sajjad. 1982. *Muslim Women and Higher Education: A Case for Separate Institutions and a Work Plan for Women's University*. Islamabad: Institute for Policy Studies.

Ahmed, Leila. 1992. *Women and Gender in Islam*. New Haven, Conn.: Yale University Press.

———. 1986. "Women and the Advent of Islam." *SIGNS* 11(4):665–91.

Ali, Abdullah Yousef. 1946. *The Holy Qur'an: Text, Translation and Commentary*. USA: McGregor and Werner.

Allen, Judith A. 1997. "Strengthening Women's Studies in Hard Times: Feminism and Challenges of Institutional Adaptation." *Women's Studies Quarterly,* 25(1,2):358–87.

Alwani, Taha Jabir Fayyad. 1993. *The Ethics of Disagreement in Islam.* Prepared from the original Arabic by Abdul Wahid Hamid. Edited by A. S. al Shaikh-Ali. Herndon, Va.: International Institute of Islamic Thought.

Amin, Sonia Nishat. 1996. *The World of Muslim Women in Colonial Bengal, 1876–1939.* Leiden: Brill.

Anwar, Etin. 2002. "Gender and Self in Islam: A Philosophical Interpretation." PhD diss., Binghamton University.

Ansell-Pearson, Keith, Benita Parry, and Judith Squires, eds. 1997. *Cultural Readings of Imperialism: Edward Said and the Gravity of History.* New York: St. Martin's Press.

Arberry, Arthur J. 1955. *The Koran Interpreted: A Translation.* New York: Macmillan.

Arjomand, Said Amir, ed. 1993. *The Political Dimensions of Religion.* Albany: State University of New York Press.

Arkoun, Mohammed. 1994. *Rethinking Islam: Common Questions, Uncommon Answers.* Translated and edited by Robert D. Lee. Boulder, Colo.: Westview.

———. 1993. *Min al-Ijtihad ila Naqd al-'Aql al-Islami.* Translated by Hashim Salih. London: Dar al-Saqi.

Arnot, Madeline. 1993. "A Crisis in Patriarchy? British Feminist Educational Politics and State Regulation of Gender." In *Feminism and Social Justice in Education: International Perspectives,* ed. M. Arnot and K. Weiler, 186–209. London: Falmer Press.

Arnot, Madeleine, and Len Barton, eds. 1992. *Voicing Concerns: Sociological Perspectives on Contemporary Education Reforms.* Wallingford, Oxfordshire: Triangle Books.

Asad, Muhammad, trans. 1980. *The Message of the Qur'an.* Gibraltar: Dar al-Andalus.

Ashraf, Syed 'Ali. 1985. *New Horizons in Muslim Education.* Cambridge: Islamic Academy; Cambridge: Cambridge University Press.

Baier, Annette C. 1997. *The Commons of the Mind.* Chicago: Open Court.

Banks, James A. 1993. "The Canon Debate, Knowledge Construction, and Multicultural Education." *Educational Researcher* 22(5):4–14.

al-Banna, Hasan. 1983. *Al-Mar'ah al-Muslimah.* Compiled and edited by Muhammad Nasir al-Din al-Albani. Cairo: Dar al-Kutub al-Salafaiyah.

Barazangi, Nimat Hafez. 2004. "Understanding Muslim Women's Self-Identity and Resistance to Feminism and Participatory Action Research." In *Traveling Companions: Feminisms, Teaching, and Action Research,* ed. Mary Brydon-Miller, Patricia Maguire, and Alice McIntyre, 21–39. Westport, Conn.: Praeger.

———. 2003. "Domestic Democracy: The Road to National and International Democracy." Proceedings of the fourth annual conference of the Center for the

Study of Islam and Democracy, Washington, D.C., May 16, 2003. http://www.islam-democracy.org/4th_Annual_Conference-Barazangi_paper.asp (accessed September 16, 2003).

———. 2002. "Al-Huwiyah al-Dhatiyah lil al-Mar'a al-Muslimah" [Muslim Woman's Self-Identity]. In *Al-Mar'a al-'Arabiyah wa Taghyrat al-'Asr al-Jadid* [The Arab Woman and Change in the New Millennium]. Proceedings of the third annual cultural symposium of Dar al-Fikr, 232–45. Al-Nisa' Shaq'iq al-Rial Series. Damascus: Dar al-Fikr.

———. 2001. "Future of Social Sciences and Humanities in Corporate Universities: Curricula, Exclusions, Inclusions, and Voice." Cornell Institute for European Studies Working Papers no. 01.1. Also, http://www.einaudi.cornell.edu/parfem/workingpaper.htm (accessed December 27, 2002).

———. 2000. "Muslim Women's Islamic Higher Learning as a Human Right: Theory and Practice." In *Windows of Faith: Muslim Women Scholar-Activists in North America*, ed. Gisela Webb, 22–47. Syracuse, N.Y.: Syracuse University Press.

———. 1999a. "Self-Identity as a Form of Democratization: The Syrian Experience." In *Democratization and Women's Grassroots Movements*, ed. Jill Bystydzienski and Joti Sekhon, 129–49. Bloomington: Indiana University Press.

———. 1999b. "Is Language the Object of Literacy among United States Female Adult Learners?" *Language and Literacy Spectrum* 9:2–16.

———. 1998a. "The Equilibrium (Taqwa)," in "Issues of Islamic Education," ed. Nimat Hafez Barazangi, special issue, *Religion and Education* 25(1,2).

———. 1998b. "The Equilibrium of Islamic Education: Has Muslim Women's Education Preserved the Religion?" *Religion and Education* 25(1,2):5–19.

———.1998c. "Arabic Language Learning: A Module of a Research-Based Computerized Curriculum." Proceedings of the Sixth International Conference and Exhibition on Multi-lingual Computing, Cambridge, England, April 17–18, 1998, 7.2.1–7.2.23.

———. 1997. "Muslim Women's Islamic Higher Learning as a Human Right: The Action Plan." In *Muslim Women and the Politics of Participation: Implementing the Beijing Platform*, ed. Mahnaz Afkhami and Erika Loeffler Friedl, 43–57. Syracuse, N.Y.: Syracuse University Press.

———. 1996. "Vicegerency and Gender Justice." In *Islamic Identity and the Struggle for Justice*, ed. Nimat Hafez Barazangi, M. Raquibuz Zaman, and Omar Afzal, 77–94. Gainesville: University Press of Florida.

———. 1995a. "Religious Education." In *The Oxford Encyclopedia of the Modern Islamic World*, ed. John L. Esposito, 1:406–11. New York: Oxford University Press.

———. 1995b. "Educational Reform." In *The Oxford Encyclopedia of the Modern Islamic World*, ed. John L. Esposito, 1:420–25. New York: Oxford University Press.

———. 1993. "Worldview, Meaningful Learning and Pluralistic Education: The Islamic Perspective." *Religion and Public Education* (now, *Religion and Education*) 20(1–3):84–98.

———. 1992. "North American Muslim Women Speak." *North American Council for Muslim Women's Newsletter* (Great Falls, Va.) 1(2).

———. 1991a. "Islamic Education in the United States and Canada: Conception and Practice of the Islamic Belief System." In *The Muslims of America*, ed. Yvonne Y. Haddad, 157–74. New York: Oxford University Press.

———. 1991b. "Parents and Youth: Perceiving and Practicing Islam in North America." In *Muslim Families in North America*, ed. Earle H. Waugh, Sharon MacIrvin Abu-Laban, and Regula Burckhardt Qureshi, 132–47. Edmonton: University of Alberta Press.

———. 1990a. "The Education of North American Muslim Parents and Children: Conceptual Change as a Contribution to Islamization of Education." *American Journal of Islamic Social Scientists* 7(3):385–402.

———. 1990b. "Acculturation of North American Arab Muslims: Minority Relations or Worldview Variations." *Journal of Muslim Minority Affairs* (London) 11(2):373–90.

———. 1989. "Arab Muslim Identity Transmission: Parents and Youth." *Arab Studies Quarterly* 11(2,3):65–82; and in *Arab Americans: Continuity and Change*, ed. Baha Abu-Laban and Michael W. Suleiman, 65–82. Belmont, Mass.: Association of Arab-American University Graduates.

———. 1988. "Perceptions of the Islamic Belief System: The Muslims of North America." PhD diss., Cornell University.

———. 1982. *Education Is the Means to Free Oneself from Shirk*. Plainfield, Ind.: Amana Trust Publication.

Barazangi, Nimat Hafez, Davydd J. Greenwood, Melissa Grace Burns, and Jamecia Lynn Finnie. (2004). "Evaluation Model for an Undergraduate Action Research Program." Conference proceedings: "Learning and the World We Want," 152–59, ed. Budd Hall and Maria del Carmen Rodriguez de France. November 20–23, 2003, Victoria, B.C., Canada. http:www.edu.uvic.ca/learning/proceedings.pdf

Barazangi, Nimat Hafez, M. Raquibuz Zaman, and Omar Afzal, eds. 1996. Introduction to *Islamic Identity and the Struggle for Justice*, ed. Nimat Hafez Barazangi et al., 1–8. Gainesville: University Press of Florida.

Barlas, Asma. 2002. *"Believing Women" in Islam: Unreading Patriarchal Interpretations of the Qur'an*. Austin: University of Texas Press.

Al Bayan. 1998. *Al-Ahadith: Al-Muttafaq alayha bayn al-Bukhari wa-Muslim*. CD-ROM, Sakhr version 2.0 by Harf. Cairo.

Ba-Yunus, Ilyas, and Moin Siddiqui. 1998. *A Report on Muslim Population in the United States*. New York: Center for American Muslim Research and Information.

Belhachmi, Zakia. 2000. "Al Sa'dawi's and Mernissi's Feminist Knowledge with/in the History, Education and Science of the Arab-Islamic Culture." PhD diss., University of Montreal.

Benhabib, Seyla. 1992. *Situating the Self: Gender, Community, and Postmodernism in Contemporary Ethics*. New York: Routledge.

Bennabi, Malek. 1968. *Al-Dhahira al-Qur'aniyah*. Translated by Abd al-Sabour Shahin (from French to Arabic). Damascus: Dar al-Fikr.

Bennett, William John. 1992. *The De-valuing of America: The Fight for Our Culture and Our Children*. New York: Summit Books.

Bluenfeld, Samuel. 1995. *Is Public Education Necessary?* Boise, Idaho: Paradigm Company.

Brand, Laurie. 1998. "Women and the State in Jordan: Inclusion or Exclusion?" In *Islam, Gender, and Social Change*, ed. Yvonne Y. Haddad and John Esposito, 100–123. New York: Oxford University Press.

Brine, Jacky. 1999. *Undereducating Women: Globalizing Inequality*. Feminist Educational Thinking Series, ed. F. Weiler, G. Weiner, L. Yates. Buckingham: Open University Press.

al-Bukhari, Muhammad ibn Ismail. 1997. *Sahih*, The Translation of the Arabic meanings into English, by Muhammad Muhsin Khan. Medina: Islamic University; Chicago: Kazi, 1997.

Bullock, Katherine Helen. 2003. *Rethinking Muslim Women and the Veil: Challenging Historical and Modern Stereotypes*. Herndon, Va.: International Institute of Islamic Thought.

Butler, Judith. 1990. *Gender Trouble: Feminism and the Subversion of Identity*. New York: Routledge.

Carnegie Council on Adolescent Development. 1995. *Great Transitions: Preparing Adolescents for a New Century, Concluding Report*. New York: Carnegie Corporation of New York.

Clancey, William J. 1997. *Situated Cognition on Human Knowledge and Computer Representation*. Cambridge: Cambridge University Press.

Cole, Juan R. I., ed. 1992. *Comparing Muslim Societies: Knowledge and the State in a World Civilization*. Ann Arbor: University of Michigan.

Cornell, V. J. 1994. "Tawhid: The Recognition of the One in Islam." In *Islam: A Challenge for Christianity*, ed. Hans Küng and Jürgen Moltmann, 1994: 61–66. London: SCM Press.

Council on Islamic Education. 1995. *Teaching about Islam and Muslims in the Public School Classroom*. Fountain Valley, Calif.: Council on Islamic Education.

Crocco, Margaret Smith, Petra Munro, and Kathleen Weiler, eds. 1999. *Pedagogies of Resistance: Women Educator Activists, 1880–1960*. Foreword by Nel Noddings. New York: Teachers College Press.

Cummins, Jim. 1999. "Alternative Paradigm in Bilingual Education Research: Does Theory Have a Place?" *Educational Researcher* 28(7):26–32.

Davies, Merryl Wyn. 1988. *Knowing One Another: Shaping an Islamic Anthropology*. London: Mansell.

Denny, Frederick M. 1989. "Fazlur Rahman: Muslim Intellectual." *Muslim World* 79(2):91–101.

DeVries, Reta. 1997. "Piaget's Social Theory." *Educational Researcher* 26(2):4–17.

Douglass, Susan L. 1995. *Teaching about Islam and Muslims in the Public School Classroom*. Fountain Valley, Calif.: Council on Islamic Education.

———, ed. 1994. *Strategies and Structures for Presenting World History: With Islam and Muslim History as a Case Study*. Council on Islamic Education. Beltsville, Md.: Amana Publications.

Dutton, Yasin. 1999. "Juridical Practice and Madinan 'Amal: Qada' in the Muwatta of Malik." *Journal of Islamic Studies* 10(1):1–21.

Eickelman, Dale F. 1985. *Knowledge and Power in Morocco: The Education of a Twentieth-Century Notable*. Princeton, N.J.: Princeton University.

Engineer, Asghar Ali. 1990. *Islam and Liberation Theology: Essays on Liberative Elements in Islam*. New Delhi: Sterling.

al Faruqi, Isma'il Raji, ed. 1986. *Trialogue of the Abrahamic Faiths*. Ann Arbor, Mich.: New Era Publications.

———. 1982a. *Islamization of Knowledge: The Problem, Principles, and Workplan*. Islamabad: National Hijra Century Committee of Pakistan.

———. 1982b. *Tawhid: Its Implications for Thought and Life*. Wyncote, Penn.: International Institute of Islamic Thought.

al Faruqi, Maysam. 2000. "Self-Identity in the Qur'an and Islamic Law." In *Windows of Faith: Muslim Women Scholar-Activists in North America*, ed. Gisela Webb, 72–101. Syracuse, N.Y.: Syracuse University Press.

———. 1998. "From Orientalism to Islamic Studies." *Religion and Education* 25(1,2):20–29.

Fawzi, Ibrahim. 1987. *Ahkam al-Irth*. Beirut: Dar al-Haqiq.

Fernea, Elizabeth Warnock. 1998. *In Search of Islamic Feminism: One Woman's Global Journey*. New York: Doubleday.

Freire, Paulo. 1981. *Education for Critical Consciousness*. New York: Continuum.

———. 1970. *Pedagogy of the Oppressed*. Translated by Myra Bergman Ramos. New York: Herder and Herder.

Gaddy, Barbara B., T. William Hall, and Robert J. Marzano. 1996. *School Wars: Resolving Our Conflicts over Religion and Values*. San Francisco: Jossey-Bass.

Garaudy, Roger. 1983. *Islam habite notre avenir*. Paris: Desclée de Brouwer, 1981; translated (from French to Arabic) by Abd-al-Majid Baroudy as *Al-Islam Din al-Mustaqbal* (Damascus: Dar al-Iman).

Gay, Geri, and Joan Mazur. 1989. "Conceptualizing a Hypermedia Design for Language Learning." *Journal of Research on Computing in Education*, winter, 119–26.

Glazer, Nathan. 1997a. "Multiculturalism Gains an Unlikely Supporter." *Chronicle of Higher Education*, April 11.

———. 1997b. "Multiculturalism, Religious Conservatism, and American Diversity." In *Religion, Ethnicity, and Self-Identity*, ed. Martin E. Marty and Scott Appleby. Hanover, N.H.: University Press of New England.

Goldziher, Ignac. 1967. *Muslim Studies* [Muhammedanische Studien]. Edited by

S. M. Stern. Translated from the German by C. R. Barber and S. M. Stern. London: Allen and Unwin.

———. 1966. *A Short History of Classical Arabic Literature*. Translated, revised, and enlarged by Joseph Desomogyi. Hildesheim: G. Olms.

———. 1961. *Encyclopedia of Religion and Ethics*. Edited by James Hastings with the assistance of John A. Selbie and Louis H. Gray. New York: Scribner.

Greenwood, Davydd J. 2004. "Feminism and Action Research: Is 'Resistance' Possible and, If So, Why Is It Necessary?" In *Traveling Companions: Feminism, Teaching, and Action Research*, ed. Mary Brydon-Miller, Patricia Maguire, and Alice McIntyre, 157–68. Westport, Conn.: Praeger.

Greenwood, Davydd J., and Morten Levin. 1998. *Introduction to Action Research: Social Research for Social Change*. Thousand Oaks, Calif.: Sage.

Greenwood, Davydd J., William Foote Whyte, and Ira Harkavy. 1993. "Participatory Action Research as a Process and as a Goal." *Human Relations* 46(2):175–92.

Grumet, Madeleine R. 1990. Foreword. In *Changing Education: Women as Radicals and Conservators*, ed. Joyce Antler and Sari Knopp Biklen, ix–xii. Albany: State University of New York Press.

El Guindi, Fadwa. 1999. *Veil: Modesty, Privacy and Resistance*. New York: Berg.

Habermas, Jürgen. 1979. *Communication and the Evolution of Society*. Translated and introduced by Thomas McCarthy. Boston: Beacon Press.

Hale, Sondra. 1999. "Women Warriors." Review of *Voices of Resistance: Oral Histories of Moroccan Women*, by Alison Baker, 1998. In *The Women's Review of Books* 16(12):20–22.

Hall, Budd. 1981. "Participatory Research, Popular Knowledge and Power: A Personal Reflection." *Convergence* 14(3):6–19.

Hammam, Mona. 1977. "Women Workers and the Practice of Freedom as Education: The Egyptian Experience." PhD diss., University of Kansas.

Harding, Sandra. 1998. *Is Science Multicultural: Postcolonialisms, Feminisms, and Epistemologies*. Bloomington: Indiana University Press.

———, ed. 1987. *Feminism and Methodology: Social Science Issues*. Bloomington: Indiana University Press.

———. 1986. "The Instability of the Analytical Categories of Feminist Theory." *SIGNS* 11(4):645–64.

Hare, Richard Marvyn. 1992. *Essays on Religion and Education*. Oxford: Clarendon Press.

Hassan, Riffat. 2003. "Religious Conservatism: Feminist Theology as a Means of Combating Injustice toward Women in Muslim Communities/Culture." http://ncwdi.igc.org/html/Hassan.htm (accessed October 30, 2003).

———. 2000. "Human Rights in the Qur'anic Perspective." In *Windows of Faith: Muslim Women Scholar-Activists in North America*, ed. Gisela Webb, 241–48. Syracuse, N.Y.: Syracuse University Press.

———. 1995. "Muslim Feminist Hermeneutics." In *In Our Own Voices*, ed. Rosemary Skinner Keller and Rosemary Radford Reuther, 455–59. San Francisco: Harper.

———. 1994. "Women in Islam and Christianity: A Comparison." In *Islam: A Challenge for Christianity*, ed. Hans Küng and Jürgen Moltmann, 18–22. London: SCM Press.

———. 1991. "'Jihad fi Sabil Allah': A Muslim Woman's Faith Journey from Struggle to Struggle to Struggle." In *Women's and Men's Liberation—Testimonies of Spirit*, ed. Leonardo Grob, Riffat Hassan, and Haim Gordon, 11–30. Westport, Conn.: Greenwood.

———. 1982. "On Human Rights and the Qur'anic Perspective." In *Human Rights in Religious Traditions*, ed. Arlene Swidler. New York: Pilgrim Press.

Haw, Kaye. 1998. *Educating Muslim Girls: Shifting Discourses*. Feminist Educational Thinking Series, ed. K. Weiler, G. Weiner, and L. Yates. Buckingham: Open University Press.

Haynes, Charles C. 1994. *Finding Common Grounds: A First Amendment Guide to Religion and Public Education*. Nashville, Tenn.: Freedom Forum First Amendment Center, Vanderbilt University.

al-Hibri, Azizah Y. 1997. "Islam, Law and Custom: Re-defining Muslim Women's Rights." *American University Journal of International Law and Policy* 12(1):1–44.

———. 1992. "Islamic Constitutionalism and the Concept of Democracy." *Case Western Reserve Journal of International Law* 1:11–13.

———. 1982. "A Study of Islamic Herstory: Or How Did We Ever Get into This Mess?" In *Women and Islam*, ed. Azizah al-Hibri, 207–19. Oxford: Pergamon Press. Also published as a special issue of the Journal Women's Studies International Forum 5,2 (Great Britain).

Hirschmann, Nancy J., and Christine Di Stefano, eds. 1996. *Revisioning the Political: Feminist Reconstructions of Traditional Concepts in Western Political Theory*. Boulder, Colo.: Westview.

Hoffman, Valerie J. 1998. "Qur'anic Interpretations and Modesty Norms of Women." In *The Shaping of an American Islamic Discourse: A Memorial to Fazlur Rahman*, ed. Earle H. Waugh and Frederick M. Denny, 89–122. Atlanta, Ga.: Scholars Press.

Hollinger, David. A. 1997. "Visiting Historian to Discuss Culture and Ethnoracial Classifications." *Cornell Chronicle*, April 24, 4.

———. 1996. *Science, Jews, and Secular Culture: Studies in Mid-Twentieth-Century American Intellectual History*. Princeton, N.J.: Princeton University Press.

hooks, bell. 1994. *Teaching to Transgress: Education as the Practice of Freedom*. New York: Routledge.

Horton, Myles, and Paulo Freire. 1990. *We Make the Road by Walking: Conversations on Education and Social Change*, ed. B. Bell, J. Gaventa, and J. Peters. Philadelphia: Temple University Press.

Houghton, Ross C. 1877. *Women of the Orient: An Account of the Religious, Intel-

lectual, and Social Condition of Women in Japan, China, India, Egypt, Syria, and Turkey. Cincinnati: Cranston and Stowe.

Hull, John M. 1998. "Religious Education and Muslims in England: Developments and Principles." *Muslim Education Quarterly* 5(4):10–23.

Ibn Hisham, Abd al-Malik. 1858–1860. *Kitab Sirat Rasul Allah.* Edited by Ferdinand Wustenfeld. Gottingen: Dieterichsche Universitats Buchhandlung.

Ibn Miskawayh, Ahmad (932–1030 AD). 1961. *Tahdhib al-Akhlaq.* Beirut: Maktabat Dar al-Hayat.

Ibn Saʿd, Muhammad. 1904/AH1321. *Kitab al-Tabaqat al-Kabir.* Edited by Brokelman. Leiden: Brill.

The Ideal Muslim Husband. 1997. Video recording. Chicago: Sound Vision Foundation.

Iqbal, Mohammad. 1962. *The Reconstruction of Religious Thought in Islam.* Lahore: Muhammad Ashraf.

Jessup, Henry Harris. 1874. *The Women of the Arabs.* Edited by C. S. Robinson and Isaac Riley. London: Sampson Low, Marston, Low and Searle.

Kahf, Mohja. 2000. "Braiding the Stories: Women's Eloquence in the Early Islamic Era." In *Windows of Faith: Muslim Women Scholar-Activists in North America,* ed. Gisela Webb, 147–71. Syracuse, N.Y.: Syracuse University Press.

———. 1999. *Western Representations of the Muslim Woman: From Termagant to Odalisque.* Austin: University of Texas Press. Also, http://campusgw.library. cornell.edu/cgi-bin/ebooks.cgi?bookid=44686 (accessed February 10, 2003).

———. 1998. "Huda Shaʿrawi's Mudhakarati: The Memoirs of the First Lady of Arab Modernity." *Arab Studies Quarterly* 20(1):53–82.

Kahhalah, Umar Rida. 1977. *Aʿlam al-Nisaʾ fi ʾalamay al-ʾArab wa-al-Islam.* Damascus: Muʾassassat al-Risalah.

Kamali, Mohammad Hashim. 1991. *Principles of Islamic Jurisprudence.* Cambridge: Islamic Text Society.

Kassis, Hanna E. 1983. *A Concordance of the Qurʾan.* Foreword by Fazlur Rahman. Berkeley: University of California Press.

Kerr, David A. 1995. "He Walked in the Path of the Prophets: Toward Christian Theological Recognition of the Prophet Muhammad." In *Christian-Muslim Encounters,* ed. Yvonne Y. Haddad and Wadi Zaidan Haddad. Gainesville: University Press of Florida.

Khurasani, Abi Tahir Tayfour. 1998. *Balaghtat al-Nisaʾ.* Edited by Abd al-Hamid Hindawi. Cairo: Dar al-Fadhilah.

Kramer, Martin S. 2001. *Ivory Towers on Sand: The Failure of Middle Eastern Studies in America.* Washington, D.C.: Washington Institute for Near East Policy.

Lahham, Hanan. 1989. *Min Hadi Surat al-Nisaʾ* [The Guidance of the Chapter "The Women" of the Qurʾan]. Damascus: Dar al-Huda.

Lewis, Bernard. 2001. "What Went Wrong: Western Impact and Middle Eastern Response." Video recording. West Lafayette, Ind.: C-SPAN Archives 2001.

Lickona, Thomas. 1997. "The Promulgation of Virtue." In *Conversation with Education Leaders: Contemporary Viewpoints on Education in America*, ed. Anne Turnbaugh Lockwood, 21–30. New York: State University of New York.

Lockwood, Alan L. 1997. "The Current Incarnation of Character." In *Conversation with Education Leaders: Contemporary Viewpoints on Education in America*, ed. Anne Turnbaugh Lockwood, 31–38. New York: State University of New York.

Lockwood Ann Turnbaugh, ed. 1997. *Conversation with Education Leaders: Contemporary Viewpoints on Education in America*. New York: State University of New York.

Lueg, Andrea. 1995. "The Perception of Islam in Western Debate." In *The Next Threat: Western Perception of Islam*, ed. Jochen Hippler and Andrea Lueg, trans. Laila Friese. Boulder, Colo.: Pluto Press with Transnational Institute.

Lugg, Catherine A. 1996. *For God and Country: Conservatism and American School Policy*. New York: Peter Lang.

Maguire, Patricia. 2001. "Uneven Ground: Feminisms and Action Research." In *Handbook of Action Research: Participative Inquiry and Practice*, ed. P. Reason and H. Bradbury, 59–69. London: Sage.

———. 1987. *Doing Participatory Research: A Feminist Approach*. Amherst: Center for International Education, School of Education, University of Massachusetts.

———. 1984. *Women in Development: An Alternative Analysis*. Amherst: Center for International Education, School of Education, University of Massachusetts.

Mahdi, Muhsin. 1990. "Orientalism and the Study of Islamic Philosophy." *Journal of Islamic Studies* 1:72–98.

Malik ibn Anas. 1951. *Muwatta' al-Imam Malik*. Cairo: Dar 'Ihya 'Ulum al-Din.

Mandinach, Ellen B., and Hugh F. Cline. 1994. *Classroom Dynamics: Implementing a Technology-Based Learning Environment*. Hillsdale, N.J.: Lawrence Erlbaum.

Matthews, Victor H., Bernard M. Levinson, and Tikva Frymer-Kensky, eds. 1998. *Gender and Law in the Hebrew Bible and the Ancient Near East*. Sheffield, UK: Sheffield Academic Press.

Maudoodi, Syed Abul A'ala. 1972. *Purdah and the Status of Woman in Islam*. Translated and edited by al-Ash'ari. Lahore: Islamic Publications.

———. 1967. *Al-Hijab*. Beirut: Dar al-Fikr.

Mayo-Jeffries, Deborah. 1994. *Religious Freedom in the Education Process: A Research Guide to Religion in Education (1950–1992)*. Buffalo, N.Y.: William S. Hein.

Mazrui, Ali. 1994. "Global Apartheid? Race and Religion in the New World Order." In *The Gulf War and the New World Order*, ed. Tareq Y. Ismael and Jacqueline S. Ismael, 521–35. Gainesville: University Press of Florida.

Mazur, Joan M. 1993. "Interpretation and Use of Visuals in an Interactive Multimedia Fiction Program." PhD diss., Cornell University.

McIntyre, Alice. 1997. *Making Meaning of Whiteness: Exploring Racial Identity of White Teachers*. Albany: State University of New York Press.

Mernissi, Fatima. 1993. *Women and Islam: An Historical and Theological Enquiry*. Translated by Mary Jo Lakeland. New Delhi: Kali for Women.

———. 1992. *Islam and Democracy: Fear of the Modern World*. Translated by Mary Jo Lakeland. Reading, Mass.: Addison-Wesley.

———. 1991. *The Veil and the Male Elite: A Feminist Interpretation of Women's Rights in Islam*. Translated by Mary Jo Lakeland. Reading, Mass: Addison-Wesley.

———. 1987. *Beyond the Veil*. Bloomington: Indiana University Press.

Metcalf, Barbara Daly. 1996. *Making Muslim Space in North America and Europe*. Berkeley: University of California Press.

Middleton, Sue. 1993. *Educating Feminists: Life Histories and Pedagogy*. New York: Teachers College Press.

Miller, S., M. W. Nelson, and M. Moore. 1998. "Caught in the Paradigm Gap: Qualitative Researchers' Lived Experience and the Politics of Epistemology." *American Educational Research Journal* 35(3):377–416.

Mir, Mustansir. 1986. *Coherence in the Qur'an: A Study of Islahi's Concept of Nazm in Tadabbur-i Qur'an*. Indianapolis, Ind.: American Trust Publications.

Moin, Mumtaz. 1997. *Umm al-Mu'minin 'A'ishah Siddiqah Life and Work*. Karachi: Salman Academy.

Morris, Barbara M. 1979. *Change Agents in the Schools*. Upland, Calif.: Barbara Morris Report.

Moustafa, Tamir. 2000. "Conflict and Cooperation between the State and Religious Institutions in Contemporary Egypt." *International Journal of Middle East Studies* 32(1):3–22.

Muhammad, Zakiyyah. 1998. "Islamic Education in America: A Historical Overview with Future Projections." *Religion and Education* 25(1):87–96.

Murphy, Richard W., and F. Gregory Gause, III. 1997. "Democracy and U.S. Policy in the Muslim Middle East." *Middle East Policy* 5(1):58–67.

Nasr, Seyyed Hossein. 1995. "Comments on a Few Theological Issues in the Islamic-Christian Dialogue." In *Christian-Muslim Encounter*, ed. Yvonne Y. Haddad and Wadi Zaidan Haddad, 457–67. Gainesville: University Press of Florida.

National Governors Association. 1993. *Ability Grouping and Tracking: Current Issues and Concerns*. http://www.maec.org/tracking.html (accessed January 1, 2004).

New English Bible. 1970. Oxford: Oxford University Press. Also on CD-ROM.

Noddings, Nel. 1993. *Educating for Intelligent Belief or Unbelief*. New York: Teachers College Press, Columbia University.

Nord, Warren A. 1995. *Religion and American Education: Rethinking a National Dilemma*. Chapel Hill: University of North Carolina Press.

Nord, Warren, and Charles C. Haynes. 1998. *Taking Religion Seriously across the Curriculum*. Nashville, Tenn.: First Amendment Center; Alexandria, Va.: Association for Supervision and Curriculum Development.

Nuʿman, Fareed. 1992. *The Muslim Population in the United States: A Brief Statement*. Washington, D.C.: American Muslim Council.

Okin, Susan Moller. 1998. "Feminism and Multiculturalism: Some Tensions." *Ethics* 108:661–84.

O'Malley, J. Michael, and Anna Uhl Chamot. 1990. *Learning Strategies in Second Language Acquisition*. Cambridge Applied Linguistics Series, ed. Michael H. Long and Jack C. Richard. Cambridge: Cambridge University.

Oxford, Rebecca L. 1990. *Language Learning Strategies: What Every Teacher Should Know*. New York: Newbury House.

Passerin d'Entreves, Maurizio, and Seyla Benhabib, eds. 1997. *Habermas and the Unfinished Project of Modernity: Critical Essays on the Philosophical Discourse of Modernity*. Cambridge, Mass.: MIT Press.

Posner, George. 1983. "A Model of Conceptual Change: Present Status and Prospect." Proceedings of the International Seminar on Misconceptions in Science and Mathematics. Ithaca, N.Y.: Department of Education, Cornell University.

Pumfrey, P., and G. Verma, eds. 1993. *The Foundation Subjects and Religious Education in Primary Schools*. London: Falmer Press.

Quraishi, Asifa. 2000. "Her Honor: An Islamic Critique of the Rape Laws in Pakistan from a Woman-Sensitive Perspective." In *Windows of Faith: Muslim Women Scholar-Activists in North America*, ed. Gisela Webb, 102–35. Syracuse, N.Y.: Syracuse University Press.

Qutb, Syed [Sayyid]. 1981. *Maʿalim fi al-Tariq* [English title: *Milestones*]. Translated from Arabic by S. Badrul Hasan. Karachi: International Islamic Publishers.

Rahman, Fazlur. 2000. *Revival and Reform in Islam: A Study of Islamic Fundamentalism*. Edited and introduced by Ebrahim Moosa. Oxford: One World.

———.1996. "Islam's Origin and Ideals." In *Islamic Identity and the Struggle for Justice*, ed. Nimat Hafez Barazangi, M. Raquibuz Zaman, and Omar Afzal, 11–18. Gainesville: University Press of Florida.

———. 1995. *Islamic Methodology in History*. 3rd reprint. Islamabad: Islamic Research Institute.

———. 1982. *Islam and Modernity: Transformation of an Intellectual Tradition*. Chicago: University of Chicago Press.

———. 1980. *Major Themes of the Qur'an*. Minneapolis, Minn.: Bibliotheca Islamica.

———. 1966. *Islam*. History of Religion Series. New York: Holt, Rinehart and Winston.

———. 1965. *Islamic Methodology in History*. Karachi: Central Institute of Islamic Research.

Renard, John. 1998. "Women as Scholars and Teachers." In *Windows on the House of Islam*, ed. John Renard. Berkeley: University of California Press.

———. 1994. "Islam, the One and the Many: Unity and Diversity in a Global Tradition." In *Islam: A Challenge for Christianity Concilium*, ed. Hans Küng and Jürgen Moltmann, 3:31–38. London: SCM Press.

Richey, J. A. 1922. *Selections from Educational Records.* Part 2. Calcutta: Bureau of Education, Superintendent of Government Printing.

Roded, Ruth. 1994. *Women in Islamic Biographical Collections: From Ibn Sa'd to Who's Who.* Boulder, Colo.: Lynne Rienner.

Rosenthal, Franz. 1960. *The Muslim Concept of Freedom.* Leiden: Brill.

Rubin, Uri. 1995. *The Eye of the Beholder: The Life of Muhammad as Viewed by the Early Muslims.* Studies in Late Antiquity and Early Islam, no. 5. Princeton, N.J.: Darwin Press.

Said, Edward W. 1993. *Culture and Imperialism.* New York: Knopf.

———. 1981. *Covering Islam: How the Media and the Experts Determine How We See the Rest of the World.* New York: Pantheon Books.

———. 1978. *Orientalism.* New York: Pantheon Books.

Sa'id, Jawdat. 1987. *Hatta Yghayru ma bi Anfusihm.* 7th printing. Abhath fi Sunan Taghir al-Nafs wa al-Mujtama' Series. Damascus: Dar al-Hijra.

———. 1984. *Madhab Ibn Adam al-Awwal, aw Mushkilat al-'Unf fi al-'Amal al-Islami.* 3rd printing. Abhath fi Sunan Taghir al-Nafs wa al-Mujtama' Series. Damascus: Al-Ansari.

El Sanabary, Nagat Morsi. 1973. "A Comparative Study of the Disparities of Education of Girls in the Arab World." PhD diss., University of California, Berkeley.

Schimmel, Annemarie. 1994. *Deciphering the Signs of God: A Phenomenological Approach to Islam.* Albany: State University of New York Press.

———. 1985. *And Muhammad Is His Messenger: The Veneration of the Prophet in Islamic Piety.* Chapel Hill: University of North Carolina Press.

Scott, Joan W., ed. 1996. *Feminism and History.* New York: Oxford University Press.

———. 1986. "Gender: A Useful Category of Historical Analysis." *American Historical Review* 91(5):1053–75.

Schüssler Fiorenza, Elisabeth. 1983. *In Memory of Her: A Feminist Theological Reconstruction of Christian Origins.* New York: Crossroad.

Shahrur, Muhammad. 2000. *Nahwa Usul Jadidah lil-Fiqh al-Islami: Fiqh al-Mar'ah; al-Wasiyah, al-Irth, al-Qawamah, al-Ta'addudiyah, al-Libas.* Damascus: Al-Ahali lil Tiba'ah wa al-Nashr wa al-Tawzi'.

———. 1990. *Al-Kitab wa al-Qur'an: Qira'a Mu'asirah.* Damascus: Al-Ahali.

Shalabi, Ahmad. 1993. *Al-Manahij al-Islamiyah: Usuluha al-Sahihah, Inhirafatuha, wujub Tashihiha, ma' Muqaddamah 'Ammah li-Mawsu'at al-Hadarah al-Islamiyah.* Cairo: Maktabat al-Nahdah al-Misriyah.

———. 1979. *History of Muslim Education.* Karachi: Indus Publications.

———. 1966. *Tarikh al-Tarbiyah al-Islamiyah* [History of Islamic Education]. Dirasat fi al-Hadhara al-Islamiyah Series. Cairo: Maktabat al-Nahdhah.

Shapiro, June, Sylvia Kramer, and Catherine Hunerberg. 1981. *Equal Their Chances: Children's Activities for Non-sexist Learning.* Englewood Cliff, N.J.: Prentice Hall.

Shepard, William. 1996. *Sayyid Qutb and Islamic Activism: A Translation and Criti-*

cal Analysis of Social Justice in Islam. Translation of Sayyid Qutb, *Al-Adalah al-Ijtim'iyah fi al-Islam.* Leiden: Brill.

Smith, Dorothy E., ed. 1999. *Writing the Social: Critique, Theory, and Investigations.* Toronto: University of Toronto Press.

———. 1990. *The Conceptual Practices of Power: A Feminist Sociology of Knowledge.* Boston: Northeastern University Press.

———. 1987. *The Everyday World as Problematic: A Feminist Sociology.* Boston: Northeastern University Press.

Smith, Jane I. 1975. *An Historical and Semantic Study of the Term "Islam" as Seen in a Sequence of Qur'an Commentaries.* Missoula, Mont.: Scholars Press for Harvard Theological Review.

Smith, Jane I., and Yvonne Y. Haddad. 1982. "Eve: Islamic Image of Women." In *Women and Islam,* ed. Azizah al-Hibri, 135–44. Oxford: Pergamon Press.

Smith, W. C. 1956. "The Place of Oriental Studies in a Western University." *Diogenes* 16, 108.

Soufi, Denis L. 1997. "The Image of Fatima in Classical Muslim Thought." PhD diss., Princeton University.

Soundvision.net. 1999. Changed to *Soundvision.com.* http://www.soundvision.com/Community/Newsletter/ArchiveView.asp (accessed February 18, 2003).

Spellberg, Denise A. 1994. *Politics, Gender, and the Islamic Past: The Legacy of 'A'isha Bint Abi Bakr.* New York: Columbia University Press.

———. 1988. "Nizam al-Mulk's Manipulation of Tradition: 'A'ishah and the Role of Women in the Islamic Government." *Muslim World* 78(2):111–17.

Stalker, J. 1996. "Women and Adult Education: Rethinking Andocentric Research." *Adult Education Quarterly* 46(2): 98–113.

Stanton, Elizabeth Cady. 1972. *The Woman's Bible.* New York: Arno Press.

Stauth, George. 1992. *Islam and Emerging Non-Western Concepts of Modernity.* Working Paper no. 180. University of Bielefeld, Southeast Asia Program.

Stewart, David Wood. 1993. *Immigration and Education: The Crisis and the Opportunities.* New York: Lexington Books.

Stewart, Philip J. 1994. *Unfolding Islam.* Reading, UK: Ithaca Press.

Strike, Kenneth A., and G. J. Posner. 1983. "Types of Synthesis and Their Criteria." In *Knowledge Structure and Use: Implications for Synthesis and Interpretation,* ed. Spencer A. Ward and Linda J. Reed. Philadelphia: Temple University Press.

Sullivan, William. 1982. *Reconstructing Public Philosophy.* Berkeley: University of California Press.

al-Suyuti, Jalal al-Din 'Abd al-Rahman ibn Abi Bakr. 1990. *Al-Durr al-Manthur fi al-Tafsir al-Ma'thur: Wa-huwa Mukhtasar Tafsir Tarjuman al-Qur'an.* Beirut: Dar al-Kutub al-Islamiyah.

al-Tabari, Ibn Jarir. 1960–69. *Tarikh al-Tabari: Tarikh al-Rusul wa al-Muluk.* Cairo: Dar al-Ma'aref.

———. 1902. *Selections from the Annales of Tabari.* Edited by M. J. deGoeje. Leiden: Brill.

Tolmin, Stephen. 1972. *Human Understanding*. Vol. 1, *The Collective Use and Evolution of Concepts*. Princeton, N.J.: Princeton University Press.

UNESCO. 1992. *Human Development Report*. New York: United Nations Development Programme.

———. 1964. *Access of Girls and Women to Education in Rural Areas: A Comparative Study*. Paris: UNESCO.

United Nations. 1995. *Women: Looking beyond 2000*. New York: United Nations.

———. 1996. *Covenant for the New Millennium: The Beijing Declaration and Platform for Action*. From the Fourth World Conference on Women. Santa Rosa, Calif.: Free Hand.

United Nations Development Programme. 2003. Arab Fund for Economic and Social Development. *Arab Human Development Report 2003: Building a Knowledge Society*. http://www.undp.org/rbas/ahdr/english2003.html (accessed November 15, 2003).

———. 2002. Arab Fund for Economic and Social Development. *Arab Human Development Report 2002: Creating Opportunities for Future Generations*. http://www.undp.org/rbas/ahdr/bychapter.html (accessed December 28, 2002).

United States Commission on Excellence in Education. 1984. *A Nation at Risk: The Full Account*. Cambridge, Mass.: USA Research.

Wadud, Amina. 1999. *Qur'an and Woman: Reading the Sacred Text from a Woman's Perspective*. 2nd ed. New York: Oxford University Press.

Wadud-Muhsin, Amina. 1992. *Qur'an and Woman*. Kuala Lumpur: Penerbit Fajar Bakti Sdn.

Waggenspack, Beth M. 1989. *The Search for Self-Sovereignty: The Oratory of Elizabeth Cady Stanton*. Great American Orators Series, no. 4. New York: Greenwood Press.

Watt, William Montgomery. 1988. *Islamic Fundamentalism and Modernity*. London: Routledge.

Waugh, Earle H., and Frederick M. Denny, eds. 1998. *The Shaping of an American Islamic Discourse: A Memorial to Fazlur Rahman*. Atlanta, Ga.: Scholars Press.

Waugh, Earle H., Sharon McIrvin Abu-Laban, and Regula Burckhardt Qureshi, eds. 1991. *Muslim Families in North America*. Edmonton, Canada: University of Alberta Press.

Webb, Gisela, ed. 2000. *Windows of Faith: Muslim Women Scholar-Activists in North America*. Syracuse, N.Y.: Syracuse University Press.

Weiler. Kathleen. 1990. "You've Got to Stay There and Fight: Sex Equity, Schooling, and Work." In *Changing Education: Women as Radicals and Conservators*, ed. Joyce Antler and Sari Knopp Biklen, 217–36. Albany: State University of New York Press.

Wild, Stefan. 1996. *The Qur'an as Text*. Edited, translated, and with a commentary by Stefan Wild. Leiden: Brill.

The World Almanac and Book of Facts. 2004. New York: Newspaper Enterprise Association.

Wulff, Helena. 1995. "Introducing Youth Culture in Its Own Right." In *Youth Cultures: A Cross-Cultural Perspective*, ed. Vered Amit-Talai and Helena Wulff, 1–18. London: Routledge.

Young, Iris Marion. 1990. *Justice and the Politics of Difference*. Princeton, N.J.: Princeton University Press.

al-Zirikli, Khayr al-Din. 1954–59. *Al- 'Alam: Qamous Tarajim*. Damascus and Cairo: Kutstomas.

Index

Nimat Hafez Barazangi is a research fellow at Cornell University. She edited and contributed to *Islamic Identity and the Struggle for Justice* (1996), and has published more than twenty-five articles, essays, and book reviews. She has received several awards for her participatory action research, including the Glock Award from the Department of Education at Cornell University for her 1988 PhD dissertation; a visiting fellowship from Oxford University; a scholarship from the International Council for Adult Education; a three-year serial Fulbright scholarship for Syria; and the United Nations Development Program 1999 and 2002 fellowships for Syria.

Related-interest titles from University Press of Florida

Against Islamic Extremism: The Writings of Muhammad Sa 'id al- 'Ashmawy
Carolyn Fluehr-Lobban

Between Cross and Crescent: Christian and Muslim Perspectives on Malcolm and Martin
Lewis V. Baldwin and Amiri YaSin Al-Hadid

Biblical Interpretation and Middle East Policy: The Promised Land, America, and Israel, 1917–2002
Irvine H. Anderson

Daughters of Abraham: Feminist Thought in Judaism, Christianity, and Islam
Edited by Yvonne Yazbeck Haddad and John L. Esposito

Emails from Scheherazad
Mohja Kahf

The Islamic Quest for Democracy, Pluralism, and Human Rights
Ahmad S. Moussalli

Islamic Societies in Practice, second edition
Carolyn Fluehr-Lobban

The Kingdom of Saudi Arabia
David E. Long

The Veil Unveiled: The Hijab in Modern Culture
Faegheh Shirazi

For more information on these and other books, visit our Web site at www.upf.com.